Beyond Buzzwords

Social Media, Mobile & Other Marketing Buzzwords Ain't the Half of It!

Foreword By Lorrie Thomas Ross

Michelle A. Bassett *&* Temitayo A. Osinubi

For information regarding special discounts for bulk purchases,
please contact Digital Marketing Advisers special sales at
+1-855-WEB-WORK
or at
ThinkBeyoundBuzzwords.com/Bulk-Deal

ISBN-10: 0-9972583-0-6
ISBN-13: 978-0-9972583-0-1

FREE Resource website at
ThinkBeyondBuzzwords.com/Resources

Cover design by
Michelle A. Bassett
Development editing by Amber Avines

Table of Contents

Acknowledgements

Michelle:

*For the teachers, friends, and family members that saw me,
not as I was, but as I am.*
                                                    -Michelle A. Bassett

Temi:

There's an old African proverb, it takes a village to raise a child. Well this child is the product of several villages, whom I would all thank individually if time permitted. However, in lieu of that allow me give special thanks to:

The mother of my children, Tiffany. Though our relationship has evolved over time, know that I will forever be grateful to you for two of the most beautiful children I've ever laid eyes on.

To my mother, Rosalind Osinubi. Thank you for raising me to be intelligent, inquisitive and articulate. I know I didn't make your job easy. I thank you for never giving up on me.

To my late grandfather, Percy Oliver Vera, thanks for being the man in my life and showing me what it looks like when a man loves his family above all else. An economics professor, you were brilliant enough to be the head of any firm on Wall St., instead you chose to invest in your community through teaching and mentorship, as well as a great deal of time in me. Your love and sacrifice was not lost on me, no matter how I acted. I will always regret not showing you how much I loved and appreciated you before you died.

For all the aunts, uncles, nieces & cousins know that I love you all, but frankly there's just too many of you to mention here! Lol!

To the IMBS/IMMS faculty at Full Sail University. Thanks for helping to bring structure to the untamed wilderness that is Digital Marketing. I want to give a special thanks to my Google Online Marketing Challenge (GOMC) faculty facilitators Rob Croll & Carol Cox. My PPC instructor, contributor to this book and all around good dude Brett Burky, as well as all of my GOMC teammates Jefferson Akly, Tiffany McDonald, Angel Brown, Nancy Folgmann and last but never least Roger Spence.

To Robert Kiyosaki of *Rich Dad/Poor Dad*. Thank you for sharing your wisdom with the world and setting me on the path of financial education. Save for the Bible, I can't think of another series of books that has had such a profound impact on my life.

Both authors would like to thank:

Our millionaire mentors Debbie and Delxino Wilson de Briano. Thank you for not just talking about improving the black community, but doing it! We want to be like you when we grow up.

To all of the industry experts who gave so willingly of themselves in the making of this book, Lorrie Thomas Ross, Michael King, Michael J. Becker, Brett Burky (again cuz you're that dope) and Kerry O'Shea Gorgone. The shining example of professionalism you've set cannot be overstated. Thank you for being willing to mentor us and allowing us to follow in your footsteps.

Last, but not least, our Success Quest mentor Chike Akua. You forever changed us for the better. With deep, deep gratitude, thank you!

Foreword

In August 2013, I flipped open my laptop to get on a Google Hangout interview with Temitayo Osinubi. He connected with me via LinkedIn to talk marketing shop for a class assignment at Full Sail University after watching my online marketing videos on lynda.com. His passion for Digital Marketing and learning was immediately apparent. Although we weren't in the same room (he was in Ohio and I was in Santa Barbara), our time in the hangout created an instant connection…that and he could hang with my all-over-the-place-ness as my entrepreneurial marketing brain went off on tangents!

I have been in this wacky, wild and wonderful web marketing world since 1999. As a recovering online ad salesperson who cut her teeth in this industry at a time when flashing banner ads and pop ups were all the rage, I can tell you that this industry has come a long, long way. Witnessing the dot-com boom, bust and now working in the thriving Digital Marketing space with a breadth and depth of options, the options for students, marketers and business owners to sink their teeth into is kind of like a honeycomb – sweet, beautiful, but sticky and complex.

Choices are great, but where the heck do you begin as you start to navigate the wild, wild web? There are a plethora of phrases thrown around by companies and professionals (and unfortunately too many un-professionals) trying to make a claim in the web world. All the Digital

Marketing buzz is very exciting, but it can also be so darn overwhelming. You don't have to get stuck or stung by the buzz. Digital Marketing overwhelm is treatable – the prescription is simple: EDUCATION.

Do you know what the two most dangerous words are? I + KNOW. After 15 years in web marketing, I can tell you that NOBODY knows everything. And we don't grow if we aren't continually learning. We get good at marketing by learning. We learn from programs (Full Sail University offers degree programs), there are countless books and online video companies that have fantastic video tutorials on any marketing subject you can imagine.

When I was studying marketing in my early college days, the 4 P's of marketing that I learned from my expensive hardback books were: product, place, promotion and price. Today, we pee on those P's! They are dated. Let me breakdown the old Ps and shed light on what I feel are the new ones:

Product: Companies don't just sell products, they also sell services. Some companies sell products and services. No matter what you sell, know that today consumers support passion over product. **Passion** is contagious. It is what creates a viral impact and keeps customers loyal.

Place: In the old days, companies needed a great location for visibility. Today, we don't need a place (I know, my company has been virtual for over a decade), we just need a presence. A powerful **presence**

is a healthy mix of web, social, personal branding, PR, email, and search. A powerful presence puts place in its place.

Promotion: While big, expensive ads used to rule, getting on the top of a mountain and screaming your brand's name isn't effective marketing anymore…it's just noise. And in a wild web world ridden with noise, the only way to cut through the clutter is to replace promotion with **pedagogy**. The method and practice of teaching is what connects consumers to companies. I am a mark**ed**ing® (marketing via education) evangelist. Respect is reciprocal. When we educate our target market(s), we empower them and when people are empowered, they feel more powerful to buy what we are selling.

Price: Competing with price is dated. Come on, are people wearing Gucci and driving Jaguars because they are a steal? Get real. It's people over price. **People** choose who and what they support based on the way that they feel – what feels right, what makes them feel right and what humans are searching for at our core is connection and that connection with consumers begins by being a person. Some brands are business to business (B2B) and some are business to consumer (B2C), but what makes companies profit is humanizing their brand, operating with a people to people (P2P) approach.

Today's 4 P's are driven by Digital Marketing: **Passion, Presence, Pedagogy** and **People**.

It has been two years since I met Temitayo through the wild, wonderful web. Thanks to the power of social media and online communication, I have been able to get to know him and now Michelle personally and professionally. It's a small world and it got even smaller when both Temitayo and I moved to Atlanta. Being able to sit down live was awesome. I could have geeked out with them for a week! I am so thankful for this industry because I get to meet wonderful people like them. They are an inspiration and a reminder of how remarkable the web is.

I have always told my students that the way to solidify what you learn is by writing it out. Temi and Michelle are walking the talk. They know Digital Marketing, they love Digital Marketing, they are lifelong learners and are so generous to share themselves and what they know in this book.

This book is a work of heart. Whether you're a 10+ year veteran or new to web marketing, this book shares experience and insight that will broaden your horizons and expand your thinking. Temi and Michelle, thank you for being so bold and courageous to connect with all the thought leaders you have and to be willing to share what you love. I carry you both in my hearts as Digital Marketing professionals and now as friends.

-Lorrie Thomas Ross

WebMarketingTherapy.com & LorrieThomas.com

Preface

Michelle's Story

Thanks for picking up this book. I'm Michelle A. Bassett and I will be one of your guides down the rabbit hole that is known as Internet Marketing.

My Internet Marketing journey started out in a very similar fashion as many other high-ranking, "new age" Internet Marketers. I was on my computer one day just minding my own business; I clicked the wrong button, and changed my life forever.

My first "Internet Marketing" experience was in 2010. I was finishing up my Bachelor's Degree in Behavior Analysis at Savannah State University, I opened an email or clicked on an ad or something like that and I wound up at a landing page for an MLM (Multi-Level Marketing) known as *Infinity Downline*. I was young, dumb and I fell for it.

Just for clarity sake *Infinity Downline* was this company where you would pay $25 a month. For every person you enrolled you got $25. The only catch was, you would lose people along the way. If memory serves me, you would lose your second and fourth person, those people would go to the person that fooled you into joining. Everyone after the "roll up period" would be yours and you would receive a monthly $25 per person under you. Pretty much it was a fancy, money-gifting program that walked the very thin line of legality. Again, to a 22-year-old with no money it seemed legit.

A motivating factor for joining was an MLM called … *sigh* … *Amway/Quick Star*. Yes, I was in that program, which I will never mention in this book again. It was late 2009, so the gateways for other Network Marketing companies were wide open. Once again, this is a NO JUDGMENT ZONE. Clearly, I didn't learn my lesson from my previous MLM experience, but it gave me knowledge of the structure of an MLM and I was already familiar with the payouts and the roll ups and everything else.

So, once I totally bombed with *Infinity Downline* and that other company; I, like any rational self-respecting adult, decided that I would leave MLMs alone for good; and that I would utilize the degree I was in the process of obtaining. At least that's what I would say if that were true. However, in reality, there is nothing further from the truth.

I went from the two programs mentioned above to other programs like *ZNZ*, all the way up to a $500 program with an additional $99 a month commitment, called *Numis Network*. Did I learn my lesson? Nope. From there, I started doing a program called *Internet Lifestyle Network*. Once that went south I joined yet another $500 company called *World Ventures*; another called *Advocare* and another company for $99 a month called *MB360*. Then it got bad, I started doing *Penny Clicks,* which is exactly what it sounds like. I paid like $20 to click for pennies. Pennies!

So, at that point I knew I had a problem. I went cold turkey for a while and kicked the habit...until. My very last program which was a system called *DS Domination* or DSD. Honestly, it really wasn't a bad company; I just couldn't drink the Kool-Aid. That goes for all of the companies I was apart of. It's not that they weren't good companies, and real people did make real money. The main problem was, after spending THOUSANDS of dollars, just to stay broke, I couldn't get over the innate predatory nature that is Multi-Level Marketing.

This isn't an attack on any MLMers, Network Marketers, Info-Marketers, etc. In fact I have learned and still learn a lot from those programs, and the leaders from those programs. Most of my knowledge about funnels comes from the funnel masters - Info-Marketers. My early personal development/exposure came from a program that sold soaps and lotions. So, again I'm not ragging on the industry. It just isn't for me, and I had to learn that the hard way. On a bright note, without those very expensive lessons, you wouldn't be reading this book right now.

On with the story...

Instead of giving up like a normal person, once more I looked inward. After realizing that I just wasn't going to drink the Kool-Aid, I knew that there had to be another way. I saw people who started out with nothing. No list, no money, no experience, no nothing. And those very same people six months later, a year later, two years later, however long it took, I saw them buying new cars and houses, whilst *I*, on the other hand, was driving around in the same '97 Mazda Protégé, moving from one run down apartment to the next.

After failure upon failure, and seeing success after success, I knew that there was a science to all of this and I was determined to figure it out. I knew in my heart of hearts that I was smarter and more talented than 90% of the people that confessed to making $20,000 a month and MORE. Plus Sallie Mae kept calling me asking about her money. So, I had to make a move; a move like no other move, a **bold** move.

I, Michelle A. Bassett, the first person to graduate from college in her family, the same person who couldn't read until the fourth grade, decided to get a Master's Degree in Internet Marketing. This move satisfied two very important issues in my life at that time.

First, it would mean I would know everything that there is to know about Internet Marketing, or at least that's what I thought. Secondly, it would mean Sallie Mae and the Department of Education would stop calling me day in and day out about my student loans.

In January of 2012 I started my Internet Marketing education at Full Sail University, and on February 8, 2013 I officially graduated (with honors) with my Master's of Science Degree, as it pertains to the area of Internet Marketing. I got a decent job at a law firm in Atlanta.

In the time frame of 2010-2014 I had exponentially expanded my skill set. I had a few degrees, I had a few certifications, I learned things like: how to build a website, how to use Photoshop, After Effects, and PremierePro (for video editing). I got into things like video marketing, meta data mining, Pay Per Click management, the ends and outs of a successful campaign, Analytics and Web 3.0 predictions. I had become a TRUE Internet Marketer. Those victories were nothing to sneeze at.

But, I still wasn't happy.

Over the years I had fallen in love with Internet Marking and the type of life it could offer. I'm not just talking about the cars, houses, clothes and fat bank accounts. I'm talking about, the ability to take a struggling mom and pop shop and make it a successful family-owned business. Internet Marketing isn't just the selfish ability to profit off of other people's poverty and ignorance; it's the ability to aid in the production of the American dream. That's the part I fell in love with and that's the part I still love.

But that's not what I was seeing on Facebook, LinkedIn and other social media platforms. All I was seeing were blackhat Info-Marketers and Affiliate Marketers pushing 2-year-old products telling people how they could turn their failing businesses into a success overnight with the push of a button. Worst yet, I was seeing Network Marketers flashing big checks and doctored screenshots of PayPal accounts, telling people their sob stories about how they were broke until they joined this company or that company. Now that I knew better, seeing the state of the industry that I truly loved was appalling and heartbreaking.

The above are the main reasons why I have chosen to be one of your guides. It sickens me to see so many people, and so many businesses are being taken advantage by predators. Predators who over promise and under-deliver; predators who attack businesses and unsuspecting bystanders with buzzwords like, "Social Media," "Top of Google," "PPC," and "Local SEO." Predators who dish out false information for quick cash. Now, not all of these predators are bad people. In fact I believe that most of these people honestly have the best of hopes and wishes for you and your bank account; they are simply misguided individuals that got a hold of some bad information. With that being said, my 5th grade teacher always used to say, "The pathway to hell is paved with good intentions."

The purpose of this book is for you to walk away with a better understanding of what Internet Marketing truly is. Now, this is not a How-to book, but you will get a few good nuggets out of the deal, and I do get very technical at times. I would like you to walk away learning how to "take things with a grain of salt," but unlike other marketing books, I'm going to teach you what "salt" is.

With that being said I'm ready to start when you are.

Temi's Story

Thanks for joining us. My name is Temitayo Osinubi, or Temi for short. Mobile marketing instructor and pioneer Michael J. Becker is quoted as saying "Marketing has changed more in the last two years than in the preceding 50," and he's absolutely, unequivocally right! However, most people's mindset regarding Digital Marketing hasn't kept up. We believe this is a huge problem that's going to lead to a deficit in professional skill sets in the near future as the industry of Digital Marketing becomes increasingly professionalized.

Now, you're probably asking yourself what qualifies me to speak intelligently on Digital Marketing at a macro level. Well, I hold a Bachelor's Degree in Internet Marketing from Full Sail University. Whenever I tell people that I get one of two very distinct reactions:

- The first is: "Wow! That's really cool!"
- The second is: "You paid how much, for what?! Oh God no, no, no, no, no! You got hustled. I wish you had told me before you paid them; you could've paid me!!! I mean you just need to follow the right people, read all the blogs you can and go for it."

And like most myths there's always a nugget of truth to that, right? There's a tiny grain of truth that people latch onto that allows the myth to proliferate. The truth is until very recently you really didn't need a degree in Internet Marketing to get a job. Frankly, the degree programs didn't exist until around 2007/2008.

If you look at most Digital Marketing professionals, and by that I mean people who derive their full-time living from Internet Marketing (I'm not talking about dabbling with a blog here or an affiliate site there) most of them have degrees in something else. The vast majority have degrees in journalism or copywriting, or they just found their way to the industry through happenstance.

Particularly when you're talking about consulting as an Internet Marketer, degrees don't matter at all! As a consultant what matters is being able to demonstrate the desired result, be it SEO, PPC, social media or whatever. There are plenty of people with no formal education whatsoever making LOTS of money as Digital Marketing consultants due to their ability to demonstrate the desired result for their clients.

It's also true that much of the curriculum in Full Sail University's degree program is commercially available at Barnes & Nobles or on Amazon.com. You by no means need a degree to pick up a Web Analytics book by Avinash Kaushik, or get a subscription to Lynda.com and learn from industry leader and Web Marketing Therapist Lorrie Thomas Ross. Not at all! However, you do need to know who these Digital Marketing marvels are in the first place, and if you're reading this book, odds are you may not.

That being said, from 2015 going forward this is increasingly becoming not the case. As the Digital Marketing industry increasingly professionalizes itself, a much broader skill set is needed than being self-taught typically provides. The "just go for it" mentality will no longer serve you on an individual level, nor the industry as a whole. It's going to lead to a big gap in skill sets for professionals needed to fill positions in this ever-expanding industry.

As of this writing, U.S. total ad spending is estimated at $187 billion, with digital accounting for just under 30% at $52.8 billion. TV still holds the lion's share of the pie, but by some estimates digital ad spend will catch up to TV as soon as 2018. If those numbers weren't big enough for you, as of 2015 global ad spending was estimated at $540 billion with digital representing 23.9% or $129 billion.

The opportunity in this fertile space is enormous, but you have to get in position! You're out to lunch if you think you can make a career in Digital Marketing simply because you can log into Facebook. This book will give you the proper mindset and resources to be able to play in this space at a high level.

Too Soon for the Movement

Now, in order to fully appreciate my viewpoint on the industry you have to go back with me to October 2012 when I first entered Full Sail University's Internet Marketing degree program. The long and the short with me are I'm basically one of those guys who has tried to earn a full-time income online since I discovered such a thing was possible. It seemed infinitely more preferable than working a 9-5 for the next 30 years, a long commute, and being forced to be around people I really didn't care for. I just login to my computer and enjoy a full-time income with plenty of free time for my loved ones.

Now, in fact what I was searching for is what would later become known as a flexjob, which is short for flexible job. These virtual positions allow you to telecommute from home in much the same fashion as you would go to college online. You just log into your computer, complete your assigned tasks before they're due, and still enjoy all the benefits and income of a full-time job; all without the long commute, office politics and other headaches associated with traditional employment.

Citrix is the parent company of GoToWebinar, GoToTraining and a bunch of other software as a service, or SaaS, applications designed to let you work, train and collaborate from anywhere. In 2009, a full seven years after I graduated high school, they partnered with *Tiny Giant* (read more about Tiny Giants starting on page 31) Chris Brogan to coin the term workshifting. This is basically the concept of transitioning from traditional jobs to the flexjobs described above. This sparked a global movement and at the end of 2013 Citrix published a white paper *Workshifting: a global research report*. In it, they report over 93% of organizations have implemented formal workshifting policies, a 45% jump over 2012.

However, at the time of my high school graduation (2002) when I entered the workforce neither the terms flexjob nor workshifting even existed, let alone were in my vocabulary. And since the proper terms weren't in my lexicon, I was unable to properly articulate them with my online search query. Instead I searched for "how to make money online."

That erroneous quest using the wrong search query inevitably led me into the warm embrace of network marketing, also known as Multi-Level Marketing (MLM), pyramid schemes or whatever you call it; as well as Info-Marketers whom I thought were Internet Marketers, but really they were just salespeople with sophisticated funnels.

That went about as well as you might expect, which is to say not very well at all! However, to its credit that experience did get me reading the right sorts of motivational and self-help books like *Rich Dad/Poor Dad*, *The E-Myth* by Michael Gerber, *The Seven Minute Manager*, and a lot of Stephen Covey stuff — God rest his awesome soul.

So even though MLM didn't work out so well for me financially, I still managed to develop excellent business acumen. Those around me would still seek me out for advice with their business endeavors. I advised my mother who is a history professor and historical biographer; I manage my high school friend and rap artist, Aryginal The Black Golden Child; and was the inaugural chairperson for the Greater Dayton Real Estate Investors Association's (GDREIA) wholesaling subgroup in 2012.

So one day while I was online promoting a wholesale deal on Craigslist, I was also doing a post for my mom's book and later on I was

21

going to book my man a show. Then it hit me like a ton of bricks that for as varied and sorted as all of these businesses were, the one thing they all had in common besides me was the use of social media for promotion. So, in fact, I was really a home-based entrepreneur specializing in online marketing. So if I was going to be a Digital Marketer anyway, I might as well get good at it, right? I mean, there's no sense in sucking at it if this was the inevitable course my career was going to take.

However, given my experience with network marketing and info-marketers, I was very wary of Gurus promising to make me a Digital Marketing rock star… after I paid them tens of thousands of dollars of course! I could sniff out an MLM from a mile away and wanted absolutely nothing to do with it. If I even thought you were pushing a business opportunity my way I would abruptly end the conversation in a heartbeat! That's how jaded I was.

So I was really refreshed when I found out there was a bona fide, accredited degree program in Internet Marketing; and that's how I found myself at Full Sail University in October of 2012. Now, my intention when joining was merely to be able to more effectively market my product or service online, whatever that may be at the moment, using social media. I was really spinning my wheels up until that point and I knew it.

Looking back in 2015 on where I was in 2012, it's really scary just how little I knew about this truly expansive industry! I often compare the industry of Internet Marketing to the Medical industry in that it's very broad and there are several areas of specialization. You can be a brain surgeon, OB/GYN, ear nose and throat doctor, family doctor etc. The same is true of professional Internet Marketing. You can specialize in SEO, PPC, Affiliate Marketing, Mobile Marketing, Social Media, Web Analytics, Email Marketing; the list goes on and on. Don't worry if you don't know any of those terms yet, you will by the end of the book—I promise!

LOVE Home Based Business – HATE False Advertising

I know based on the previous section some might get the impression we're anti-network marketing (MLM) or anti-info-marketing, but that's not, repeat NOT the case. We love entrepreneurship in all its forms. **We're anti-false advertising!!!** These industries in particular suffer from more than their share of bold-faced liars.

As ethical, professional marketers we have zero tolerance for these types of shenanigans. This is why we say the types of things we say about the MLM and info-marketing industries. They're chuck full of sleaze balls that take "salesman speak" as a license to be professional liars. They overstate false claims like it's a sport!

At the turn of the century before last, so the 1800s going into 1900s, there was this soda company that purchased the formula to a cola. This cola went on to become one of the largest, most well respected brands in the world. However, back around 1915 when the laws around advertising were much looser, this leisurely beverage was presented as having medicinal benefits. That's right! They pushed cola as medicine! This sugary beverage with negligible health benefits, other than the adverse ones of course, was actually marketed as being good for you.

Now, in fairness and full disclosure, the medical doctor who came up with the original formula for this cola intended it as an alternative to opium (cocaine). He had been wounded in the First World War and his severe injuries made him turn to opium for pain relief. So this cola was in fact invented as an alternative to being strung out on cocaine, which is why the original formula infamously contained trace amounts of it.

Now all that being said, I happen to be a fan of this brand of cola. Me being me, I like mine with a little (or a lot) of Jack Daniels in it. But when I drink my Jack & *Cola* I'm fully aware of the health implications. I'm not suffering under any delusions of it being healthy for me. I know full well that neither the cola nor the whiskey are good for me, but choose to drink in moderation anyway simply because I like it.

However this isn't the case for the vast majority of the people who find themselves in network marketing (MLM) or info-marketing companies. The charlatans within these industries (and there are some in every industry) prey upon their distributors' ignorance and/or desperation. As a result they burn through distributors as though they were cigarettes. That's a major reason the MLM industry suffers from a greater than 90%

attrition rate, as noted by Jon M. Taylor, MBA, PhD., of the Consumer Awareness Institute in the FTC report *The Case (for and) against Multi-Level Marketing.*

But they're not cigarettes! They're people whose dreams of entrepreneurship and financial independence more often than not turn into nightmares. Personally, I was never able to fully justify looking someone in their eyes, asking them to both believe in and follow me so that their financial dreams can become a reality, while knowing full well there was a 90% probability they would fail and lose money instead of make it. So yeah, we have a pretty negative outlook on most of the operators in these industries—most, but not all!

There are good network marketing companies out there. Again, there are dirtbags in every industry, it's just these two industries in particular seem to be chock full of them. And just like there's nothing wrong with enjoying Jack & Cola in moderation, there's nothing wrong with supporting a network marketing company whose products and vision you believe in. If you've found such a company, which is a true diamond in the rough, we implore you to hold onto it with both hands.

To this day, I purchase products from network marketing companies as a supporter. If I identify with and believe in the mission of the company, I'll support it financially with my consumer dollars. But again, the rose-colored glasses are off. I know full well what I'm doing, and more importantly what I'm not doing. Not everyone in those industries can say the same, which is where we take issue.

Mindset Over Tactics (Tool Agnostic)

What we seek to convey in this book is not only an accurate snapshot of the industry as a whole as of 2015/2016, but also strategies for success if you choose Digital Marketing as a career. Like any good strategy, ours is device or tool agnostic. Regardless of which platform, mobile device or marketing tool you choose, the concepts still hold the same. So while this book may seem esoteric at times, it's because we're trying to impart a mindset and a mentality moreso than just a bunch or tactics; half of which won't work the next time Google updates its algorithm... which is something a blackhat will never tell you by the way, but more on that later.

Robert Kiyosaki, author of the number one best-selling personal finance book of all time *Rich Dad/Poor Dad: What The Rich Teach Their Kids About Money That The Poor And Middle Class Do Not*, is famous, or infamous depending on who you ask, for challenging the status quo and making bold statements such as "Your house is not an asset." He redefined the terms assets and liabilities, as well as introduced many new concepts such as "cash flow" into lexicons where they previously weren't.

Now, this was not without blowback and its share of controversy. He notably got into a Twitter beef with fellow financial Guru Suzie Orman, and filed bankruptcy on one of his companies. But regardless of what you think about Robert Kiyosaki personally, something that's not up for debate is that he forever changed the conversation around personal finance. If you ask self-made, successful people around the world what one book changed their lives, besides holy texts such as the Bible and Quran, you're going to hear *Rich Dad/Poor Dad* more than a few times.

Michelle and I seek to do something similar with the industry of Digital Marketing. A lot of good people with good intentions think they're doing Digital Marketing the right way, but remain fundamentally ignorant of the industry as a whole. These gaping holes in their professional skill set cause havoc in the industry.

It's our goal to address and correct this way of thinking, just as Robert Kiyosaki has done with *Rich Dad/Poor Dad*. Again, regardless of what you think of the man personally, to his credit he's highly skilled at taking people with ZERO financial education, and are frankly dumb when it comes to money, and bringing them into the financial intelligence conversation. That subtle skill is to be commended and cannot be overstated.

I first read *Rich Dad/Poor Dad* shortly after graduating high school somewhere around 2003/2004, and in the ten plus years since then my relationship with his works has evolved. I've grown more sophisticated about the types of advice I accept and don't blindly hang onto every word he writes or says anymore. But I can say if I hadn't read his book(s), I would not have started down the path of financial education and gotten to where I am now. It's our hope and intent to start you down the path of truly understanding what Internet Marketing is, what it isn't and giving you an accurate portrait of this very, VERY broad industry.

It's not all about social media! It's not all about mobile either. There's a lot of moving parts, it's fairly complex and is getting more complex by the day. Anybody telling you they can make you a wiz-kid millionaire with social media, all you have to do is pay them X amount of dollars… buyer beware!

So this buzzing beehive known as Digital Marketing goes far, far deeper than most people fathom. That's what we're going to address in this book. Hopefully by the time you're done reading this you won't be subject to the "ooh shiny syndrome" that runs rampant within the industry. Folks get caught up on buzzwords like social media, mobile etc. and so on. They tend to see things from a very myopic view and really don't appreciate all of the moving parts that go into being a professional digital marketer. If we've done our job, by the end of this book you will have a more accurate view of the industry of Internet Marketing as of 2016 and beyond.

Thank you for picking up this book. Again this book is more about mindset and building the proper context. Now don't get me wrong! We're going to hit you with a lot of good, meaty content as well, it's not all fluff. As a matter fact, we do our best to mitigate fluff! But just so that we're clear, our intent with this book is to change your mindset around Digital Marketing just as *Rich Dad/Poor Dad* changed people's mindsets around personal finance and financial education.

1

Tiny Giants

"Internet Marketing is still the
Wild West, but the law is coming to town."

-By Kerry O'Shea Gorgone,
MarketingProfs.com

The following is the definition of a term we created for the purposes of this chapter. No need to look it up in a dictionary, cuz you won't find it there!

Tiny Giant: An esoteric, bona fide Big Dogg Rock Star or "giant" in their given field. However if you were not in the field you'd have absolutely no clue who the heck they are i.e. Avinash Kaushik, Chris Brogan, Mark Schaefer etc. are all Tiny Giants.

It's only fitting I start the chapter about Tiny Giants by talking about my experience getting a bachelor's degree in Internet Marketing from Full Sail University, as Full Sail itself is one humongous Tiny Giant. For those who don't know, Full Sail University is a well-respected digital media school. Its graduates run the gamut in the entertainment industry from one mixing Pharrell Williams' platinum song *Happy*, to another working on popular video games franchises such as *Call of Duty*, *Halo* and *Grand Theft Auto*; as well as many movie blockbusters including *The Avengers*, *X-Men* and *The Hunger Games*. From *The Emmys* to *American Idol*, *Grey's Anatomy*, *Scandal*, *How to Get Away with Murder*, professional sporting events in the NBA, NFL, MLB and everywhere in between; there isn't too much of the entertainment business a Full Sail grad doesn't touch in some capacity.

And then you have us lowly Internet Marketers, by far the black sheep of Full Sail University. We may work in the entertainment industry or we might work at a bank. Who knows? Just about everyone needs Internet Marketing services nowadays so we aren't limited to one industry. At best we're about five-percent of the student body. Really, it's probably closer to around three-percent, but it's my story and I tell it how I want; so I say the number's five-percent.

One of the first things you should know is that not everyone is on board with the idea of a degree program in Internet Marketing. There is a school of thought that feels the industry of Digital Marketing changes too frequently to be taught in a University setting. They think everything you learn will be antiquated the moment you graduate and that you're much better off just reading all the books and blogs you can on the topic, as opposed to investing 28 months and $57,000 in tuition like I did. I wrote a more condensed article about it on my blog: http://goo.gl/pj8fqg. I invite you to leave a comment and have further discussion with me there.

While there is some truth to that, in so far as many of the textbooks in the curriculum are commercially available at Barnes & Noble or on Amazon, the real fallacy in that line of thinking is it assumes that you're receiving dated information from the halls of academia by virtue of it being taught through a University. I can assure you nothing is further from the truth! Most, if not the entire faculty at Full Sail University's Internet Marketing Bachelors of Science/Internet Marketing Masters of Science program have their own Digital Marketing agencies where they actively service clients. So it's not like they're passively talking about an industry in which they don't actively participate.

Secondly, many have worked for Disney, ABC, ESPN etc., really large international conglomerates that know what they're doing online. So this notion that once you graduate all the principles you learned become obsolete due to new information is pure fallacy. I mean, should medical or law practitioners cease going to medical or law schools because of new medical discoveries or new Supreme Court rulings that set new precedents? When put in that context, I hope you can see why this line of thinking makes no sense.

As a practical matter, they tell you from day one you'll be learning about this rapidly evolving industry forever, and if you're not down with being a lifelong learner then this industry, let alone the program, probably isn't the path for you. The above use of the word practitioner was quite purposeful, the root of the word being **PRACTICE!**

But I do understand $57,000 for a degree in Internet Marketing is a lot of money and you may be in a life situation where that just isn't possible at the moment. I really do understand! 836 days, which is equivalent to two years, three months and 13 days is the difference between when I initially attempted to enroll at Full Sail to when I actually started class.

Enrollment Details	
Campus	**Full Sail University**
Program	**Internet Marketing B.S. - Online**
Status	**Active**
Enroll Date	**7/ 9/ 2010**
Start Date	**10/ 22/ 2012**

I had poor credit at the time and needed a co-signer, sadly mine also had poor credit, so I couldn't get in. It took me two and a quarter years to get that situation sorted out and improve my financial situation.

So as our gift to you just from spending your precious time and money reading this book, we're going to pimp out your reading list with just a small snippet, a smidgen of some of the books in Full Sail University's curriculum from these Tiny Giants. You ready?

- *The New Rules of Marketing & PR* by David Meerman Scott
- *Content Rules* by Ann Handley and C.C. Chapman
- *Optimize* by Lee Odden
- *Web Analytics 2.0* by Avinash Kaushik

Finally, and this is a big one, there's this marvel of a marketer named Lorrie Thomas Ross. She's the author of *The McGraw-Hill 36-Hour Course: Online Marketing*. While her book was not in the curriculum, there's this amazing site called Lynda.com that has online video courses on just about anything you can imagine from web design to mobile marketing and more (note: Lynda.com was acquired by LinkedIn.com in April 2015); that's where I discovered Lorrie. We got assigned to watch Lynda.com courses a lot as homework, including several of Lorrie's online marketing videos.

Get a subscription to Lynda.com NOW! It's a really great value for the money. Take everything by Lorrie Thomas Ross and I can guarantee your Digital Marketing career is set on a firmer foundation than 90% of marketers today.

That's brings up one main benefits of going to Full Sail and the title of this chapter; all these great books I just gave you from these Tiny Giants; **I didn't** **know** **about** **ANY** **of** **them** **before** **coming** **to** **Full** **Sail** **University!** Furthermore, if not for Full Sail I may never have found them, or at least not hold them in such high esteem. Just because the thought leaders exist does not in fact mean you can find them!

So this notion that you can just search these folks out and you'll find them with little to no difficulty really is quite dated. You may or you may not! For some folks it's going to be harder than others based on many factors, including their browser history. Full Sail University aggregates the best Digital Marketing information on the web and keeps you safely away from some of the darker places on the Internet with their blackhat trickery and tomfoolery.

Killer Bees – Killer Content!

When it comes to bees, you have honey bees, bumblebees and even carpenter bees. And then you have killer bees, which as their name implies, are known to kill it! So too are the industry experts we've interviewed for this book; they kill it!

Throughout the book we've reached out to thought leaders who were gracious enough to share their awesomeness. Their unique perspective is truly buzzworthy. We know you'll love our killer bees' killer content.

Killer Bees – Killer Content: Kerry O'Shea Gorgone

Not long after starting class at Full Sail University in October 2012, BestOnlineUniversities.com published their Top 100 Web-Savvy Professors for 2012. Full Sail University proudly boasted three positions:

#79 Kenneth Cossin: @kenneth_cossin

#82 Rob Croll: @rcroll

#88 Kerry O'Shea Gorgone: @kerrygorgone

Naturally I made it a point to follow all 100 on the list! Prior to that, the only Full Sail professor on this list I wasn't following was Kerry O'Shea Gorgone. Kerry taught in the master's program, so as an undergraduate there weren't many natural opportunities for us to interact (the same is true of Rob Croll, however as the program director of both the IMBS & IMMS degree programs, as well as my 2012/2013 Google

Online Marketing Challenge faculty facilitator, I interacted with Rob quite often, though we never had class together).

Soon after following Kerry I learned she hosted the *Marketing Smarts* podcast by MarketingProfs.com. I became an avid listener. Many of the ebooks on my Amazon Kindle are as a direct result of listening to her podcast. I was heartbroken when she left Full Sail to work at Marketing Profs full-time. I playfully jabbed her on Twitter from that point on, referring to her as "The Deserter" and Ann Handley, Chief Content Officer at Marketing Profs and co-author of the above-mentioned *Content Rules*, as "The Professor Usurper." It was all in good fun, of course.

An intellectual property attorney by trade, in addition to her professional social media experience, Kerry was a featured expert on the May 5th, 2015 airing of *NBC Nightly News*, following the May 2nd, 2015 Mayweather - Pacquiao fight and the live stream copyright infringement controversy surrounding it. People used live streaming apps Meerkat and Periscope to broadcast the pay-per-view fight for free online, which others paid $100 for. This violated the copyright of the fight producers, who then sued both the apps themselves, as well as the individuals who used them to stream the fight. Being both an intellectual property and social media issue, this fell squarely in Kerry's area of expertise.

As host of the Marketing Smarts podcast, Kerry gets to interview some bona fide heavy hitters in the Digital Marketing space, many of whom I would never know about without her podcast a.k.a. Tiny Giants. I reached out to Kerry for her take on how the industry of Internet Marketing is increasingly professionalizing, given her unique vantage point. She was kind enough to grace us with the chapter's *Killer Bees – Killer Content*:

Kerry O'Shea Gorgone Interview:

Temitayo Osinubi = TO   **Kerry O'Shea Gorgone = KOG**

TO: When did you begin Internet Marketing professionally?

KOG: I got into marketing during graduate school, when I had an internship at a Cambridge startup called MediaMap. I won't say how long ago that was, but let's just say "mail merge" was all the rage. The Internet became part of my marketing career when I was with the marketing and communication department at Bentley University in Waltham. We started posting the alumni magazine online, and also started using student blog posts to help prospective students get an idea of what campus life was like. We started using Flickr to share photos, and claimed our name on the major social networks as they emerged.

TO: What was the professional atmosphere like then?

KOG: The Internet at that point was a little like the Wild West. No one was exactly sure what the rules were, but academia was extra careful when it came to posting. Not too many academic institutions were pushing the envelope on Facebook or trying anything too daring on their blog!

TO: How has it changed since then?

KOG: At this point, there's no way to give prospective college students a tiny sliver of insight, carefully curated from a handful of top student ambassadors at your college. They're going to get the real story (and there are as many real stories as there are students online). Embrace transparency, because you're already operating in full view of students, parents, prospects, donors…everyone!

TO: How did you find yourself teaching Internet Marketing at Full Sail University and hosting the Marketing Smarts podcast? What was that journey like?

KOG: If it were possible to answer this in three words, I'd say "lots of luck," but of course there was more to it than that. I moved from Boston to Orlando in 2008, which meant leaving my marketing job and part-time teaching. My job hunt in Florida brought me to Full Sail, where they were launching a new Entertainment Business program and needed an attorney to teach intellectual property to undergraduate students online and on campus. My experience in business, law, and teaching made me the perfect fit, so I started at Full Sail in 2008.

Two years later, I transferred to the Internet Marketing Department to teach New Media Marketing online. It turns out, my background in marketing—and my experience as a blogger and podcaster—made me well suited to teach New Media Marketing, with the added benefit of a legal perspective to minimize potential liability risks involved in online promotion. My own success using Twitter and other social networks to share content since I started teaching sealed the deal for me!

One thing that was challenging was that I wanted to attend marketing conferences to learn more about the latest thinking in the field. Unfortunately, these conferences tend to be very expensive, so I started submitting guest articles on industry sites like Marketing Profs, Social Media Explorer, and Mark Schaefer's marketing blog (goo.gl/fJWIJh).

Once I had a few articles on major sites, I was able to get press passes for events like SXSW Interactive and Content Marketing World, which enabled me to grow my network. As an added bonus, contributing to well respected sites helped me to gain exposure in the industry, and established my personal brand as an expert in the fields of social media, marketing, and law.

One of the things I liked best about teaching was the chance to bring some of the marketing experts I met to speak with students, sometimes in person and sometimes via webinar. C.C. Chapman visited campus and spoke to students when his book *Content Rules* (co-written with Ann Handley) came out, and Mark Schaefer, Sean Gardner, and Chris Brogan all did webinars for Full Sail students. I really enjoyed the Q&A portions of these events, and happened to mention to Ann Handley how much I liked interviewing.

A few months after we'd had that conversation, the managing editor of Marketing Profs left for another job. He'd launched the Marketing Smarts podcast, so now they needed a new host. Ann remembered what I said, and invited me to take over the show. I was beyond excited! I had never done my own post-production on an audio podcast before, but I sure wasn't about to say no. I gave myself a crash course in Camtasia (an editing program) and since then I've done an episode each week, talking with people like Scott Stratten, Mack Collier, Gary Vaynerchuk, and so many other fantastic, smart marketers. I absolutely love my job!

TO: You get to interview several enterprise level Internet Marketing leaders as host of Marketing Smarts. There are several mega-trends affecting the industry including mobile, big data, connected living, social media and more. Given your many interviews, which would you say affects the professional Internet Marketer most and why?

KOG: My visceral reaction is to say mobile, because the radical shift in how people consume content will impact every aspect of marketing: content has to display correctly on mobile, functionality for your site has to work across platforms, purchases need to be frictionless, whether made on a desktop computer or a smartphone. The other trend gaining traction is data and personalization: people expect businesses to remember them once they've purchased, even once. They respond to personalized, customized online experiences, and businesses that don't tap into the power of data to provide those experiences will lose out to those that are willing to invest the time and money to give the people what they want.

TO: Given your many interviews do you think large corporations are aware of the existence of Internet Marketing degree programs, or do they prefer to train their Internet marketers in-house?

KOG: Whether corporations are aware of Internet Marketing programs is difficult to say. I'd imagine individual managers might know about those kinds of programs and see their potential, while others think that a "degree in Facebook" is silly.

Smart companies value training and professional development for marketing professionals, because they know that keeping their team current is the only way to stay competitive for the long term.

The reality is that there's an entire generation of marketers currently working who have little appreciation for newer channels like search and social, but their firm grasp on the basic principles of marketing can greatly benefit junior employees, who may be "digital natives," but lack a comprehensive education in marketing. Modern marketing education should include an introduction to new channels, but also to the entirely new way of thinking the Internet has wrought: people don't respond to sales copy anymore, they respond to relevant, helpful content, delivered to them when and where they need it.

TO: Do you see this trend continuing in the future? Why or why not?

KOG: There will always be people who resist change, and there will always be those who embrace it. I absolutely think online training and education is the future, and blended learning—involving both online and in-person training—will prove effective and practical as global organizations strive to keep their marketing teams up to date.

TO: How many tools would you say you use e.g. Hootsuite, Google Analytics etc.?

KOG: Including collaboration tools for my job at Marketing Profs, which is a remote organization, I probably use 25 different tools. I don't use them all daily, but I use them with some regularity. Basecamp, Google Drive, Google Analytics, TweetDeck, Buffer, Sococo virtual office, Skype, SocialBro, Twitter analytics, AwesomeNote, IFTTT, and so many more.

TO: What's your favorite tool and why?

KOG: No tool works unless you use it as part of a bigger strategy, but the tool I find most helpful is the Buffer app. You can integrate it with SocialBro to schedule posts at the times you typically get the most engagement. I still reply to people and share things in real time, but if I know I have a podcast coming out, I want to make sure and share it several times the day it airs, to take advantage of the initial interest. (You can read up on the SocialBro and Buffer one-two punch here: goo.gl/WURMe2)

TO: Has the cost of professional marketing tools gone up or down?

KOG: Depends who you ask! There's been a rise in freemium products, which give entrepreneurs a number of options for social media monitoring, engagement, analytics, and so on. There are also more robust solutions that can power sophisticated CRMs and help brands to create and curate content, sharing it with different audience segments. The cost of these tools is not insignificant, but whether it's gone up or down, I couldn't say. The price for a system like that will vary based on the size of the organization, number of users, reporting options selected, and lots of other factors.

TO: How would you describe the state of the Internet Marketing industry today?

KOG: Internet Marketing is still the Wild West, but the law is coming to town. Opportunities abound for savvy businesses that are willing to experiment with new platforms, but they need to be smart about things like disclosure, copyright, and privacy.

TO: Do you prefer the "good old days" of marketing or are the best days still ahead in your opinion?

KOG: The best days are ahead, always, because the technology is getting more and more powerful. Some of the brightest minds in the marketing industry would admit that they couldn't achieve the same level of success today doing it the way they did: things are always changing. What makes you a great Internet Marketer is passion, curiosity, and a willingness to take risks in order to forge a genuine connection with your audience.

TO: Where would you advise the beginner to start in this brave new world of mobile marketing, business intelligence and big data?

KOG: Jump in. C.C. Chapman has often talked about how he got his degree in Computer Information Systems. He doesn't have a degree in marketing, but he co-wrote one of the most popular content marketing books ever—*Content Rules*, co-written with Ann Handley. Don't limit yourself. If you have a passion for Internet Marketing, get an education that teaches you marketing principles and fundamentals. Learn the tools, but don't get too wedded to them, because they change all the time.

TO: As data continues to proliferate at an increasing rate, in your opinion is it reasonable to think you can market online without formal training?

KOG: You can do anything without formal training, but it will take you much longer to get good at it. Investing in education for marketing—or whatever your chosen profession is—is a much smarter use of your time, generally speaking. People attend college (or go to Full Sail or seek training from MarketingProfs) to gain access to seasoned experts who will serve as mentors. These impartial, helpful professionals have only one motivation: to help you reach your potential as a marketer.

Trying to get someone to sit down with you and share information on a less formal basis is a great way to form a relationship, but you can't expect the same level of attention and dedication from an industry peer or mentor as you can from a professor or trainer. When you first start building your network, you really want to avoid putting a strain on those relationships. You may need those connections to help you later on in your career.

Takeaways

- You can be HUGE, yet small at the same time.

- Change is no excuse not to get properly educated.

- Internet Marketing is still the Wild West, but the law is coming to town.

For additional resources and content updates, please visit
ThinkBeyondBuzzwords.com/tiny-giants

2

Education Built On Sand

"When the music changes, so does the dance."

-African Proverb

In this chapter I'll be discussing three commonly held beliefs that may leave you vulnerable to being taken advantage of when it comes to online marketing. Now, the common thread tying everything together and what I want you to keep in the back of your head, is that this is NOT 10-15 years ago. Something I've noticed as I've spoken at different events and talked to small business owners about online marketing, is that while the industry has changed tremendously in a very short period of time, people's mindsets regarding Internet Marketing haven't. This is what leaves you open to being taken advantage of.

1. It's quick and easy to get on the first page of Google.

While there is some truth to this, by far the quickest and easiest way to get on the first page of Google is to pay for it! Because generally speaking, pay per click advertising or PPC, where you pay to have your ads posted at the top and right-hand side of the search engine results page, or SERP, is easy; while search engine optimization (SEO) where you try to influence the search engine's ranking of your organic listing is hard.

The reason I say this is because at its core SEO is basically reverse engineering. The only people who know, who really know, exactly what's in Google's algorithm work at Google; and they ain't telling! It's a proprietary trade secret, similar to how in its 125-year history, only a handful of executives have ever known the exact formula to Coca-Cola. Not only that, but Google is constantly tweaking that algorithm! The big announcements like Penguin, Panda and Hummingbird are just a few of the more publicized tweaks that warranted naming.

There's hundreds of thousands of little tweaks and adjustments that Google does everyday that nobody knows about. While the industry of search engine optimization has gotten increasingly professionalized in recent years, and is a lot easier to do; it's still going to take between three and six months, if not longer, to optimize your organic listing and get you ranked on the first page.

You should be very, VERY weary of anybody saying they can get you on the first page of Google organically in an unreasonably fast amount of time, like a couple of days. On the off chance they can actually deliver on that hefty promise, they're almost certainly using blackhat tactics.

Now for those of you who don't know, a blackhat tactic is any sort of tip or trick where you're basically gaming the system and operating outside of the terms of use of whatever platform you're on. You're living very dangerously with blackhat tactics because here's the thing; THEY WORK! But you know the old saying; everything is fine... until it isn't.

True story: A classmate of mine in the degree program was an affiliate for electronic vapor cigarettes or vapes. So the vapor cigarette company brought in this rock star Guru that taught the affiliates a bunch of blackhat SEO tactics. My buddy, who lived in New York, got his organic listing to the first page of Google just like the Guru promised... then Google's Penguin algorithm update came along and he was promptly de-indexed! Meaning Google completely dropped his listing from their ecosystems. One day he's at the top of the mountain, the next his organic listing simply ceased to exist.

But here's the thing; he didn't know he was doing anything wrong! He was just doing what the Guru instructed him to do. So you have these so-called Gurus out here pushing blackhat tactics, but what they're really doing is taking advantage of the dated notion that you can just put up a website and get huge amounts of traffic to your business. "Build it and they will come," right? Wrong!!!

And 10-15 years ago in the late 90s, early 2000s this was true. But again, this is not ten years ago. Outdated tactics like keyword stuffing and merely having a website simply won't cut it. Google is very good about dropping the hammer on tricksters who attempt to outwit them.

I'm a pretty smart guy and I can figure out most things online, but I don't have a PhD in Computer Science. Google employs entire teams of PhDs and data scientists whose sole purpose is to sniff out blackhat activity and eliminate it; we're talking straight-up seek and destroy squads made of some of the smartest nerds on the planet. Take my educated opinion on this one and just don't! Whatever ill-gotten gains will be extremely short lived.

2. You can drive massive amounts of traffic to your site for FREE using social media and viral videos.

Oh, the good ole' viral video myth. Michelle addresses this in detail in chapter 5, but there are two parts to this that I quickly want to address in regard to this mindset.

First, going viral; I liken it to finding your soulmate. While there are certainly things you can do to help that process along, like keep yourself together and as attractive as possible, at the end of the day you'll either find the one or you won't. There will either be a true, lifelong connection or there won't be. When you're talking about genuine affinity and attraction, be it love or online content, you can't force it.

So when it comes to viral content, there are certainly things you can do to give your content legs and thereby increase the likelihood of it going viral, just like there are things you can do to increase the likelihood of finding your one true love. But there's no way to artificially make something "go viral."

Anybody claiming they can make your content go viral, or get you 100,000 views on YouTube overnight or whatever, be very cautious. In the case of an enormous amount of views on a YouTube video in particular, they are almost certainly using bots. You can go to websites like Fiverr.com and pay to have people get views for your video. But here's the thing; BOTS DON'T BUY!!! It looks really nice, and you have a whole bunch of views, likes and shares or whatever that don't mean anything because it's contrived. What's the point of paying to have your content look great but still be flat broke? That's like a Ferrari with no engine.

The second part of this is that you can drive huge amounts of traffic via social media for free. Again part of that is true, but during the first half of 2014 around March/April, Facebook altered its algorithm to limit organic reach on business pages. So if you have a business page on Facebook, which they highly encourage, they don't want you using your personal page for business purposes, they just ratcheted back your business page's reach to near zero. In other words, the free Facebook ride is over. We've officially entered into the age of pay-to-play in social media.

Jay Baer, author of the book *Youtility: Why Smart Marketing is About Help not Hype*, articulates this sentiment beautifully over on the Convince and Convert blog with his article, *It's Time to Own Your Social Community* (goo.gl/8Wr0Ky).

Ten plus years ago when Facebook was first incepted people were finding huge amounts of success for their businesses because everything was new. Everyone, including Facebook, was still figuring out the platform. For the umpteenth time, this is not ten years ago! They've figured out the platform. They know how to monetize it. You can still get massive amounts of traffic on Facebook, but guess what? You are going to have to pay for that!

3. You don't need any type of training to be a professional Internet Marketer.

That's actually 100% TRUE, just like you don't need any professional training to cook for a living. But just because you can dunk fries at McDonald's or make a sandwich at Subway, don't make you no Bobby Flay.

As an industry, Internet Marketing is extremely fractured. By that I mean there's no one-way to become an Internet Marketer. For example, if you want to become a medical doctor, go to medical school; if you want to become a lawyer you go to law school. With Internet Marketing you can just put up some crappy WordPress site, set up your social media profiles, get a landing page and an auto-responder and BOOM! Just like that you're an Internet Marketer.

And while this low barrier to entry makes it quick and easy to start an online business, the flip side of that coin is that there's a gigantic, glacial, GARGANTUAN expanse between what you would consider a real professional Internet Marketer, be they self-taught or professionally trained, and frauds posing as Internet Marketers.

Now don't misunderstand or take that outta context, I'm not snobbish when it comes to training. I don't think everybody has to a get degree in Internet Marketing like I did. Quite the contrary, I'm openly jealous and wish to God I were smart enough to make a living doing this at a high level without having to borrow $57,000 from the U.S. Department of Education! But I'm not… and in my experience neither are 90% of the operators in the industry. I commend those who didn't need it, but most people need some form of structured education.

The importance of structured education in today's Digital Marketing environment can't be overstated. Unstructured, haphazard learning is education built on sand. With a weak foundation like that there will forever be holes in your skill set as true understanding eludes you. However, if you're Google Adwords certified, if you're HootSuite certified and you've actually taken the time to learn your craft at a professional level; I salute you and praise your commitment. More power to you! But this notion that you can just fire off and learn all there is by following the right people on Twitter is pure folly!

Here's the thing; following the right people on Twitter is huge, but you have to know whom to follow! The ugly truth of the matter that a lot people don't tell you is you're just as likely to run across a network marketing company or Info-Marketers, as you are legit thought leaders, which is what happened to me and countless others.

Times Have Changed: Web 2.0 …

The way the web used to work 10-15 years ago; again, late 90s early 2000s, is that your search results were largely keyword-based, meaning the search engine results were focused around the query itself without considering external factors. This led to the unfortunate practice of keyword-stuffing, where people would cram in as many keywords as possible to the point where the content didn't make sense when an actual human being tried to read it.

Contrary to that, the way the social web works now with Web 2.0, is that the search engine will bring back the information they have about the keyword itself and combine it with the information that they have of **YOU** as a person; so your browsing history, the communities or groups you're in, what you watch on YouTube etc. So my search results won't be the exact same as your search results, for the exact same term because our browsing behavior and who we're connected to in our online social graph is different.

So if there are a lot of network marketers or Info-Marketers in your circles and you start searching for ways to make money online (when what you actually want is a flexjob, but are unable to properly articulate that); you're just as, if not more likely to come across Info-Marketers or an MLM as you are FlexJobs.com.

So yeah, technically you can just search out the right thought leaders but please don't fool yourself into thinking that the journey isn't fraught with peril and littered with landmines, because it is! Structured education takes all the guesswork out of the equation. You'll never have to worry about any blackhat techniques or pyramid schemes being passed off on you. Every principle you'd learn at Full Sail University or a similar program is tried, true and thoroughly vetted.

In a previous chapter I gave you just a snippet of some of the curriculum in Full Sail University's IMBS program. I'm not going to do that this time. This time I'm going to give you a screenshot of my personal reading list.

But just so that you know, most, if not all of the books on my reading list are as a direct result of listening to podcasts. Two in particular I highly recommend are the *Social Pros* podcast by the above mentioned Jay Baer and the *Marketing Smarts* podcast by Marketing Profs, which is hosted by former Full Sail professor and last chapter's **Killer Bees - Killer Content** contributor Kerry O'Shea. Kerry, an intellectual property attorney by trade, used to teach in the Master's program before she was spirited away by the professor usurper Ann Handley. Shout out to the professor usurper Ann Handley! Her book *Everybody Writes* is da-bomb-dot-com and simply oozing with awesome sauce. You should pick it up immediately.

I hope illuminating these commonly held beliefs about Internet Marketing helped prepare you to really distinguish between real Internet Marketing and the get rich quick schemes. I don't want you to be an easy target.

Temi's Kindle Reading List

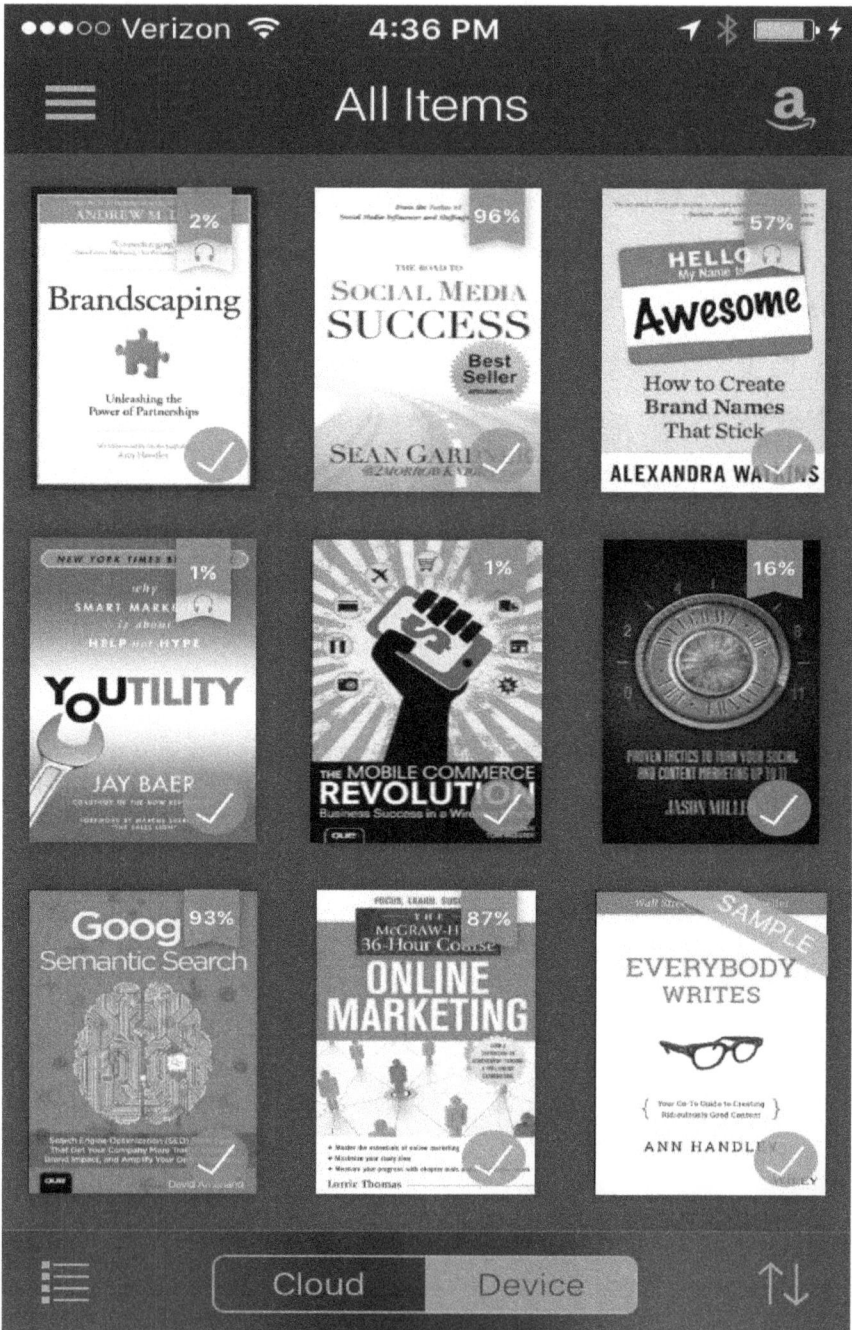

All Items

Brandscaping — 2%
Unleashing the Power of Partnerships
ANDREW M. ✔

THE ROAD TO SOCIAL MEDIA SUCCESS — 96%
Best Seller
SEAN GARD ✔

HELLO My Name is Awesome — 57%
How to Create Brand Names That Stick
ALEXANDRA WATKINS

YOUTILITY — 1%
NEW YORK TIMES B
why SMART MARKI is about HELP not HYPE
JAY BAER ✔

THE MOBILE COMMERCE REVOLUTION — 1%
Business Success in a Wir ✔

— 16%
PROVEN TACTICS TO TURN YOUR SOCIAL AND CONTENT MARKETING UP TO 11
JASON MILLE ✔

Goog Semantic Search — 93%
Search Engine Optimization (SEO) That Get Your Company More that Brand Impact, and Amplify Your O
David Amerland ✔

ONLINE MARKETING — 87%
FOCUS. LEARN. SUCC
THE McGRAW-H 36-Hour Course
Master the essentials of online marketing
Maximize your daily time
Measure your progress with chapter quiz
Lorrie Thomas ✔

EVERYBODY WRITES — SAMPLE
Your Go-To Guide to Creating Ridiculously Good Content
ANN HANDL ✔

Cloud | Device

All Items

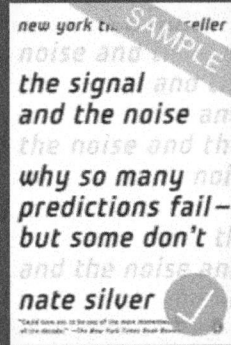

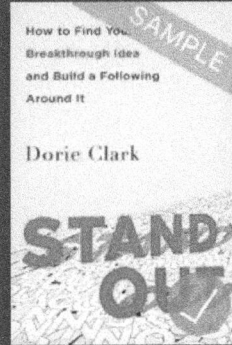

Cloud   Device

Takeaways

- This is not 10 years ago.

- Build it and they will NOT come!

- Beware blackhat tactics!

- Going viral can't be forced.

- Professional Digital Marketing DOES require an educational investment.

For additional resources and content updates, please visit
ThinkBeyondBuzzwords.com/digital-marketing-myths

3

Welcome to Pay-To-Play

"Here's how I think of my money
- as soldiers -
I send them out to war everyday.
I want them to take prisoners
and come home, so there's more of them."

- Kevin O'Leary

I hate to break it to you, but the good ole days of building a website or updating a social media post and having hundreds of engaged viewers, frantically looking for their debit cards to purchase from you online, are long gone. So are the days of blackhat SEO tactics like keyword stuffing, paying backlinking sites, and link jacking.

Before you SEO-ers start your book burning party, there's nothing wrong with SEO. There.

Now that that's out of the way, I always tell people that the quickest way to get to the number one spot in Google is through pay per click (PPC); instead of 90 days of arduous copy writing, backlinking, and doing SEO that may or may not work. In 48 hours you can have a first page top spot placement for keywords that your target audience is searching for. Which one sounds better to you? I can't hear your response, but hopefully you picked the second one.

With that being said, welcome to the reality of pay-to-play.

Let's get down to the basics of Digital Marketing and that's ads. There are many types of ads you can buy and they all garner different results. The types of ads I'm going to focus on in this chapter are:

> Text Ads
> Banner Ads
> Video Ads
> Ad Networks

Text ads are the standard text-based ads that look like Google search results. They have the blue heading with the black text and sometimes the green display URL. See example below.

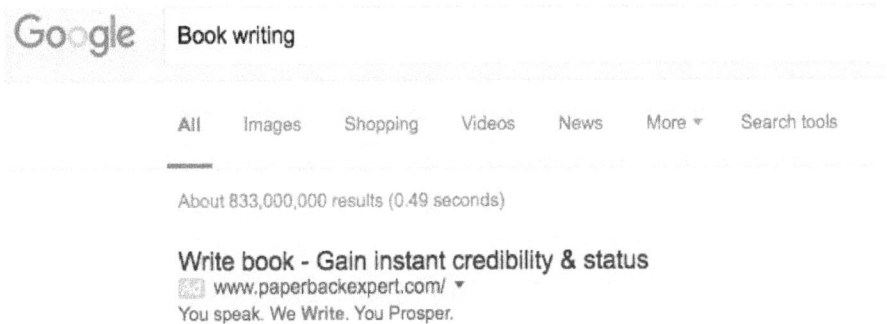

As basic as this ad form is, it is still effective at driving traffic. With these types of ads you are going to make sure that:

- Your target audience is receptive to text ads.
- You have no grammatical or technical errors.
- It sets the expectation of the product or service offered on the landing page.
- Character counts (The number of letters, spaces, punctuation, etc. allowed in an ad.)

Banner ads are visual ads that you would typically see at the top of websites, in the bottom center, or on the right hand side. See example below.

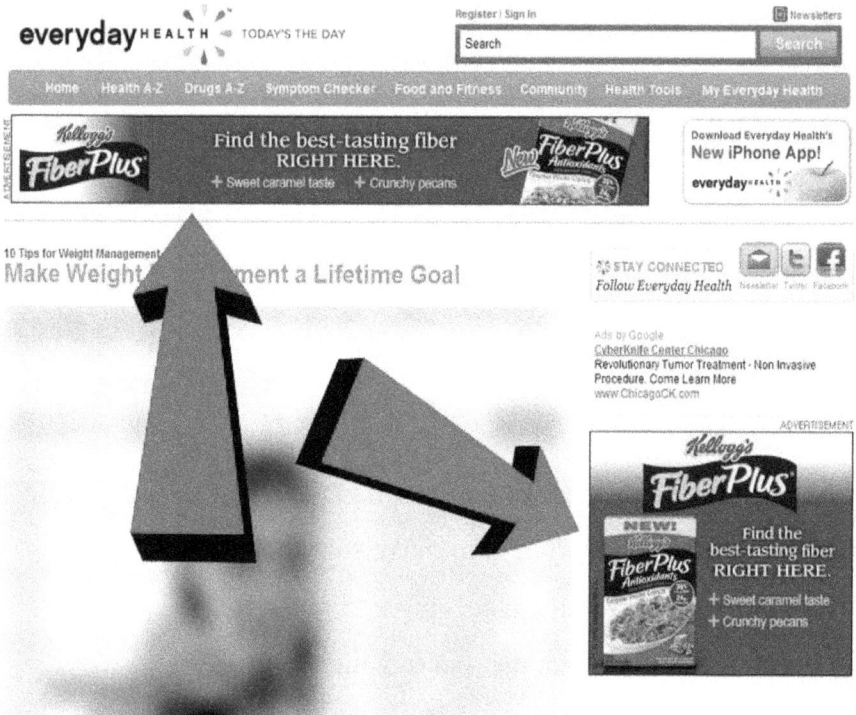

Like when you are on Facebook and you see those images in the lower right hand side, or if you are on YouTube and see that box in the upper right hand side, those are examples of banner ads. Banner ads are great for driving traffic and for branding campaigns. The most important things to have in mind when creating your banner ads are:

- The size and position of the ad.

- Using a compelling image.
- Ensuring the image is audience appropriate, both for the target audience and the website(s) displaying the ad.

Video Ads are much like banner ads, except you mostly find them on video hosting sites like YouTube, Vimeo, DailyMotion, or in front of other videos (you know, like the commercial you see before that adorable cat video). You'll also see video ads when playing mobile games and you are running out of jewels and the only way to get more is to watch a paid advertisement. We've all had to either wait five seconds to hit "skip" or wait 30 seconds for the video ad to end on its own. The important things to remember when making your video ads are:

- Gab the visitors' attention in the first three seconds, or they will skip your ad.
- Take comfort in the fact that if they do skip your ad, you don't pay.
- Make sure your targeting is set correctly when you place the ad.
- If you are advertising on mobile make sure your website is mobile friendly.

Ad Networks are much like social media networks in the sense that they are owned and operated by different people who have chosen to display your ad on their website; for a small profit, of course. The most popular ad networks are Google Adsense, The Yahoo/Bing ad network,

Outbrain and Buy-Sell-Ads. These four ad networks cover the gamut of anyone's advertising needs. The only one I didn't touch on was adult media buys. If you are selling adult content or material using a cost per acquisition (CPA) network, something like Odigger would work best for you.

Now that you know what the different ad types are, it's time to put your money where your mouth is, and start the bidding process. In the following chapters I am going to focus on PPC, PPV, and CPA. I know it's just a bunch of letters right now, but knowing the difference can make or break a marketing budget.

Pay Per Click, or PPC, is when you pay every time someone clicks your ad. This could be a few cents or a few dollars depending on the keyword and the ad network. This type of bidding is for people whose goal is to drive traffic, and ultimately have the user buy a product or service. You typically see these ads when you do a search on any major search engine. Because you are paying per click, if you don't set and keep an eye on your budget you can quickly lose money.

Pay Per View, or PPV, is a bidding method that is based on the impression or views for your ad. This can be a banner ad or a video ad. This works best for branding campaigns. To further define these terms, "an impression is a single display of a particular ad on a web page..." (goo.gl/l9hZiG). On the other hand a view can be defined as, the digesting of content. This could be in the form of clicking an ad to read an article, all the way to not hitting the "skip" button on a Youtube ad. Unlike PPC, PPV can have a set cost; where you pay per thousand of views.

Cost Per Acquisition, or CPA, is when the advertiser only pays when an acquisition is made. This doesn't necessarily mean that they bought something. This could mean a user filled out a contact form or opted into a subscription-based service.

<Related side note> If you are looking to make extra cash, joining a CPA (cost per acquisition) program may help offset some of your own marketing costs. By placing other people's ads on your own website, you can pay for your *own* marketing. A lot of people look at me funny when I say such things, but this is no different than working an 8 to 5 job and running your own business on the side. It's the same thing. *</Related side note>*

When consulting or blogging the question that always come up is, which paid advertising method should I be using? Anyone who knows me well knows my favorite answer to these types of questions. "It depends."

"So, Ms. Bassett, what does it depend on?"

I thought you'd never ask.

First things first, you always have to think about what you are trying to accomplish. Are you trying to build a brand or get people to buy a product? If you are building a brand then PPV using a media-based ad network is what I'd suggest. If you want people to buy a one-time product that's less than $500, then PPC may be your best fit. On the other hand if you are selling a product that's more than $500 and/or it has a membership aspect that exceeds that threshold, then CPA is your way to go.

Of course, nothing is set in stone. Every situation is different, and for that reason I always suggest using a combination of Paid Ad Strategies. For example, car dealerships may want to use all three. It's not just because they have thousands of dollars to blow on marketing each month, but because in their very competitive field all three of those methods apply to them.

As a dealership owner you want to get your name out there. You want to make sure that people know that they can trust Cheap Unicorn Car Depot of Atlanta to provide them with a reliable car that will last them for years! For that, you are going to need a branding campaign that is set to more general settings and reaches a broad audience in a targeted area. Next you are going to want to appear at the top of the search engine results page (SERP), when a user types in best cheap auto dealer Atlanta. As mentioned in the beginning of this chapter the fastest, most efficient way to do that is through PPC. In that campaign you'll start to push the buyer through the car-buying funnel. Some will push through the funnel, others won't and that's ok. Lastly, as a car dealership owner your focus is to get potential car buyer information, like email addresses, telephone numbers, type of car they are looking for, etc. The fastest way to get them to that part of the funnel is with an acquisition method like CPA.

So thinking back to the question, now that you have a better view of what each method does, which one or combination will work best for your business or product?

Terms to Know (see page 204)

Campaign

CPC

Impressions

CPM

CTR

Landing Page

Keywords

Match types

You are just dangerous enough to go out in the world and start a PPC, PPV, or CPA campaign now. However, this is just one honeycomb in a hive of hundreds. Now that the ads are done, and ready to go live make sure the following things are done with mastery:

- The ads are going to the correct URL.
- The URL that the ads are going to works.

- The display URL that the ads are going to matches the destination URL.

- The landing page is optimized for conversions. I know this is a big one… See resource site for tips and tricks.

And that's it. You now have enough information to drive paid traffic to your website. Have fun. Once you get comfortable, visit the analytics chapter of this book to learn how to lower your ad cost while improving your overall ROI (that means return on investment).

Takeaways

- PPC, PPV, and CPA are different ad types.

- Note that there is more than one way to bid on your ads.

- Use multiple ad and bidding strategies to figure out which one works best for you.

For additional resources and content updates, please visit
ThinkBeyondBuzzwords.com/pay-to-play

4

Facebook is Plan B;
Your Website Is Plan A

"If you don't have a seat at the table,
you're probably on the menu."

-Elizabeth Warren

In this chapter I'll be discussing why nothing, and I do mean **nothing**, takes the place of having a website. Over-relying on social media in general, but Facebook in particular, is not the best idea. But in case you missed it in Chapter Two, Jay Baer of Convince & Convert wrote a masterful blog post as only he can, *It's Time to Own Your Social Community* (goo.gl/8Wr0Ky). Yes, I'm repeating myself but this bears repeating. I highly recommend you check it out, but to sum it up with an excerpt:

"What if you shifted your strategy away from trying to use leased social to recruit, retain, and reach your audience on leased social, and instead used leased social to recruit your most enthusiastic supporters to join you in a community that you own?"

What follows is a real life example as to why this is so important. I originally hale from Dayton, OH, which is approximately halfway between Cincinnati and Columbus, OH. In 2014, the University of Dayton Men's Basketball team caught national media attention for busting everyone's bracket and making it all the way to the Sweet 16. 2014 was our Cinderella season, as it were (Go Flyers)! Later that year my hometown would catch national media attention again, but for a less inspiring and more tragic reason.

In August 2014, in the Dayton suburb of Beavercreek OH, 22-year-old John Crawford III was shot and killed by police inside Walmart while shopping for a toy gun. Someone made a prank 911 call accusing Mr.

Crawford of brandishing the weapon at shoppers. Surveillance cameras showed Mr. Crawford did nothing of the sort and was merely shopping, however he was killed within seconds of police engaging him; not unlike 12-year-old Tamir Rice who was shot dead by Cleveland, OH police a mere two seconds after they engaged him.

For whatever reason Mr. Crawford's story hasn't received as much sustained media coverage as the Mike Brown, Eric Garner and Freddie Gray incidents. The media did talk about it of course, but it hasn't received as much **sustained** media coverage as the other high profile police killings of unarmed black men.

If I were a betting man, I would bet because this particular police killing happened inside of Walmart, that Walmart had a hand in downplaying this story. I watch a lot of Discovery Channel, Travel Channel etc. and when I do choose to engage in politics, MSNBC. As a professional marketer I noticed some very curious media spend from Walmart during that holiday season. It's out of character for Walmart to run commercials on *The Rachel Maddow Show*, regardless of it being Christmas or not. That type of program usually garners media spend from Edward Jones, Rolex and the like… not Walmart. The consumer profiles or personas simply aren't aligned. However, I noticed a conspicuous media spend from Walmart virtually everywhere that holiday season, regardless if it was consistent with their consumer profile or not. One might suspect because they were embroiled in a PR disaster, courtesy of a prank call and a trigger happy Beavercreek, OH police officer, but that's just speculation on my part.

Point of Clarification It is not my intent to proselytize, polarize or piss-off anyone with this rather provocative example. This is a book about the current state of Digital Marketing, not social activism. I chose this personal example first and foremost because it happened in my community; but moreover, it speaks to the disconnect between the conventional wisdom of using social media to achieve business objectives, and the implementation needed to make it happen. I've found this disconnect is as pervasive in grassroots non-profits as it is with small to medium size businesses (SMBs).

It's like when people casually advise you to diet and exercise to lose weight. What does that mean, specifically? Which diet; high metabolism, juicing, Primal/Paleo, gluten free etc.? Exercise how; weight lifting, walking, running, Zumba etc.? This conventional wisdom, be it exercise or social media, is intended to convey meaning but doesn't actually mean anything when you really get down to it. So if the issue of this unarmed black man being slain by law enforcement for merely being a consumer is too poignant for you, simply substitute your favorite nonprofit or small business and you'll find the principles work all the same.

Anyway, as you might imagine we in the Dayton, OH community were rather upset about this! So one evening I saw a notice for a community meeting regarding this tragedy on Facebook. I joined the

Facebook group and went to the community meeting to see what would be done from a civil disobedience standpoint.

When I arrived I was struck by two things:

- While this non-profit was rather skilled at garnering media attention and getting on the evening news, there wasn't much marketing infrastructure on the back-end to facilitate getting the message out.
- There was a near total dependence on Facebook from a marketing standpoint.

This is not, repeat NOT a criticism. I'm merely reporting what I saw.

As a student working towards a bachelor's degree in Internet Marketing, I volunteered to help build out their marketing infrastructure. One of the first things was getting a free email auto-responder, Mail Chimp, set up so that they could send out CAN-SPAM compliant emails. Email has its own chapter in this book, but it bares mentioning here that the CAN-SPAM Act stands for the:

Control
Against
Non-
Solicited
Pornography
And
Marketing

It's the law governing commercial emails. There can be fines up to $16,000 per email sent, so it's very important to stay compliant, even and especially for a 501(c)(3) non-profit. I also suggested Call Loop for commercial SMS text messaging to get people out to events etc.

An over reliance on Facebook to get their message out wasn't the best thing from a strategic standpoint for several reasons, but here are the top three:

- **A website gives you better analytics:** If you rely mainly on private Facebook groups to communicate your message, while the tracking is good it still doesn't compare to having a website, in my opinion. When someone lands on your website you know how they got there, how long they were on the site, when they left, etc. So you have a bunch of metrics on your website in terms of measurement and engagement that you don't get with a Facebook group. And remember, if it can be measured it can be improved.

- **A website provides additional means to disperse your message:** You can have an online pressroom or online media room where you publish videos, articles and press releases. You can package your message in such a way that news stations will just grab it and run with it. You really can't do that to the same degree with a Facebook group, especially a private one.

But the main reason you don't want to rely on Facebook primarily for communicating with your audience is:

- **You're basically renting your audience from Facebook:** The audience that you created, that you worked so hard to build; Facebook still owns it because ultimately it's their platform. So you have to rent your audience back from them!

Jay Baer, (I'm a huge fan of his. Does it show?) wrote extensively about "Reachpocalypse" (Reach + Apocalypse = Reachpocalypse) on the Convince and Convert blog: *This Chart Explains the Reachpocalypse and Why Facebook is Laughing All the Way to the Bank* (goo.gl/bcmFDq).

For business pages, Facebook has basically gotten rid of organic reach. You can still reach people on Facebook but guess what, you're gonna have to pay to do that! It makes sense because Facebook is a publicly traded company now. They have a fiduciary responsibility to their investors to produce return and they accomplish this by selling advertising.

I observed that while community leaders understood the value of social media and the power of their message going viral; they didn't necessarily understand how to give their content legs to facilitate that happening. In addition to sharing on social media, you need back-end systems such as an email auto-responder (MailChimp), commercial SMS text message marketing platform (Call Loop) and customer relationship management (CRM) systems in place (we use WordPress).

For argument's sake let's say you do a YouTube video and it actually goes viral. Boom! You get 50 million views overnight. Now what? What do you want people to do?

- Join your email list?
- Download your app?
- Volunteer on the weekend?
- Show up for a protest?
- Make their own user generated content (UGC) around your cause, like the ice bucket challenge videos?
- Write their congressman?
- Write a check?

These are all very different outcomes, which require different marketing tactics. Clearly there's more of a commitment involved in writing a check versus hitting the like button.

So this dated notion of just putting stuff on Facebook and hoping that it goes viral is not a real marketing strategy. If anything it's a proper waste of an opportunity. In the unlikely event the content actually does go viral, if the peripheral things aren't taken care of you can't capitalize on it.

I hope in this short chapter I was able to get across why nothing takes the place of having a website. Over-relying on Facebook is not the best route strategically, and lazy marketing quite frankly. Facebook may be the biggest, but no longer the best for freebies.

If you're stuck in 2006 and expecting to market for free on Facebook you're sadly mistaken. Facebook is absolutely monetizing their platform. There has to be a call to action (CTA) funneling people to a digital property you OWN and have control over. There is no substitute for this and will facilitate your message spreading like wildfire.

To be clear, I still recommend Facebook as an advertising platform. Marty Weintraub of aimClear, a dominant audience targeting agency out of Minnesota, sums it up best "If you sit down and treat the Facebook UI (user interface) as a global demographic, psychographic profiling tool you will be stunned at the audiences you can target."

Facebook is the largest voluntary organization in history. They're highly skilled at collecting enormous amounts of information about their users, making its consumer targeting second to none. But again, the moment Facebook went public the free ride was officially over. The good news is it's a heck of a lot cheaper than a Super Bowl ad, and you get more bang for your marketing spend buck! But free... not anymore.

Below is a quick checklist of marketing infrastructure needs that should be met in order to get your message spreading like wildfire.

Marking Infrastructure for Non-Profits Checklist

- ☐ A place to house content – website, blog
- ☐ Content
  - o Text
  - o Images
  - o Videos
  - o Testimonials
- ☐ Make it look pretty
  - o Professional
  - o Donation worthy
- ☐ PayPal account
  - o Donation button on website
  - o If you don't have a website, use an email address to collect PayPal donations.
- ☐ Auto-responder
  - o Automatically sends pre-written timed emails after people "opt-in" to your list.
- ☐ Drip campaign – The actual content that goes into the auto-responder mentioned above. Content is "dripped" over a period of time e.g. 7-10 days after they opt-in. Also known as a boot camp.
- ☐ Commercial SMS text platform e.g. CallFire
  - o For example text "donate" to 12345 to pledge $5

Takeaways

- The free ride is over!

- Facebook is officially a paid channel now.

- Stop renting what you built.

- Your website is still the center of your digital universe.

- Facebook is still the best audience targeting money can buy!

For additional resources and content updates, please visit ThinkBeyondBuzzwords.com/owned-media

5

Wanna Go Viral?

"If you do not know how to ask
the right question, you discover nothing."

-W. Edwards Deming

Generally in life when it comes to the term viral it's usually not a good thing. On the Internet however, it means something a little different. According to the *Michelle A Bassett Dictionary of Terms and What Nots,* viral is defined as:

A piece of digital content that spreads rapidly throughout the consciousness of the Internet. This content is circulated by digital users with little to no regard for geographic, cultural, racial, and/or educational boundaries.

Basically a video, article or another piece of content is shared, usually through a social network, and is shared by hundreds or thousands of people.

Examples of viral campaigns would be "The Ice Bucket Challenge," another would be "Grumpy Cat," and yet another would be the "Black Lives Matter" campaign. You could find examples of viral events almost everywhere in pop culture. There are whole TV shows based off of viral Internet content. The *America's Funniest Home Videos* digital equivalent is a TV show called *Tosh.0*. Another good example is an MTV show called *Ridiculousness.*

At least once a month, if not once a week, I have someone ask me, "How do you make that go viral?" Instead of answering their question I usually ask them, "Why do you want that to go viral?" I typically get a blank stare, and a rebuttal that has nothing to do with their content going viral, not even bacterial for that matter...did you get it? "Viral"... "bacterial"...never mind.

In my experience most people who want something to go viral don't understand three basic things about what they are requesting. Those things are:

1. What viral is?
2. What it takes for content to explode all over the Internet.

     Lastly and most importantly, and as demonstrated above,

3. Why do they want their content to go viral?

You, however, are one step ahead of the game. You already know the definition of *viral*, at least the definition according to me. So, let's move on to the second one, what is takes for content to explode all over the Internet.

Spread Like a Wildfire

The Elements of Online Sensationalism

The content itself

In order for a piece of content to go viral it would have to be made up of the following elements:

Unique

Unexpected

Emotional

    Funny

    Inspirational

Short

How it spreads

Kevin Allocca, YouTube's trends manager did a 2011 Ted Talk called "Why Videos Go Viral." He mapped out the following scenario:

Tastemakers, people with large audiences that can influence them to do or not to do something, share the content. Then that content is consumed and "played with" by the community. This play is usually in the form of "remixes" or meme creation. In order for the first two things to happen the original piece of content must be unexpected in some way. So, it would have to be original, unique, and emotional, as I stated above. The meme below is of a very intense charter from a once popular American TV show called the *Jersey Shore*.

THATS CLEARLY

A GOOD MEME

imgflip.com

The dark side of viral content

Just like all things in life, having tons of people looking at your content has a downside. Well, it has lots of downsides, but I'm only going to focus on the following:

You can't focus on the people that would truly engage with your content (ie, target audience), because you've casted your net too wide. When this, let's say video, goes viral according to the definition it *"spreads rapidly throughout the consciousness of the Internet… with little to no regard for geographic, cultural, racial, and/or educational boundaries"*. So, how much of your target market do you think you'll hit? Better question, what is the percentage of people who will see this video and not buy your product? 98%, 99%, 99.9%? Even a better question, and probably the best question ever asked in life: How much of your target market will you reach and how many of them will be turned off by your video? 80%? 90%?

Getting viable sales from viral content is possible, but when it does happen, it happens in a short spike. This revenue spike can also be referred to as a bubble. Just like the housing market bubble popped in the early 2000s, the viral content bubble will eventually pop; and if you are not prepared for this, it will crash your business.

Lastly, if your viral content was branded correctly it has your logo and brand name all over it. This doesn't sound like a bad thing, but what happens when someone, for no other reason besides they live a miserable life, decides that they don't like your product. If you have a food item, what if they say they tried it one time and they got food poisoning? If it's a lotion, what if they say it gave them a rash or you test your products on baby seals? If you have electronics, software, or an online service what happens when Mr. Miserable tells the world that because of your product their company failed? What do you do then? The answer to this obviously rhetorical question is: nothing! Once it gets out you can do absolutely nothing about it. Their lies may snowball out of control and possibly destroy your business' reputation.

"So what do I do instead?"

So, why do you want your content to go viral again? If you are a traditional children's pastry chef in Austin, TX; why do you want a 60-year-old, cake hating, vegan in West Palm Beach, FL looking at your content? Truly think about what that does for your business. If you are purely seeking fame and brand placement, then there is a possibility that you may want your content to go viral. But for most small business models, having uncontrollable content roaming free on the Internet is not what they want. By all means, if after reading this chapter you do want your content to go viral, use the principles above and make it happen. If you are in the 90% of readers whom now have no interest whatsoever in going viral then continue on to the next paragraph.

Instead of aiming for infecting the Internet with mind numbing foolishness, aim to feed your target market with rich wholesome content.

If you are in fact a children's pastry chef in Austin, TX, (wow what are the chances!) or if you are not a children's pastry chef in Austin, TX, I still want you to answer the following questions:

- Who is your target market?

- Where do they like to hang out online?
- What kind of content would they like to receive? Said another way, what type of material would they opt into your email list for?

Let me help you out. Your target market is probably going to be, either mothers with kids ages 3-10 or professional party planners, which in essence are the same thing. For this example I'm just going to focus on the moms. Next, where do they hang out online? Probably places like Pinterest, blogs about parenting, and crafting sites. What kind of content would these people sign up for? Content with beautiful images of colorful kids' cakes that's about how to bake and decorate cakes with your kids for a special occasion? If you produced a fun kid-friendly, how-to, monthly, video directed at Austin moms with great party ideas, you'd be able to brand your business, grow a huge following, and make tons of consistent money.

On the flip side of this, if your unrelated fluff-filled content went viral, you may make a few bucks, but you can't aim that content at your target audience (buyers), and your revenue would be inconsistent, making it almost impossible to grow and scale your business.

I know that was a lot to take in. Here's the condensed version. Having a piece of content go viral is a good thing if you are looking for a quick boost or spike in traffic. It's not good if you are trying to grow and sustain a business. The best thing to do when creating content for your business is to think about what your target market really wants, and give it to them on a consistent basis.

Takeaways

- You miss your target audience the majority of the time when you make content for the majority of people!

- Give your audience what they want, when they want it.

- Building a profitable sustainable brand is about rich content not viral content.

For additional resources and content updates, please visit
ThinkBeyondBuzzwords.com/going-viral

6

Video Marketing: Fast, Cheap, and Easy

"If a picture is worth a thousand words then a video is worth a thousand pictures."

-Michelle A. Bassett

According to a 2013 study carried out by the U.S. Department of Education, 14% of the U.S. adults cannot read. That 14% represents roughly 32 million adults. For those that have attained some level of literacy, 21% of those adults (48 million) read below a 5th grade level.

As a person who quietly suffered with a reading disability all throughout elementary, high school, undergraduate and graduate school these numbers come as no surprise. Which should be less of a shocker to you is that, **people who do not read well tend not to read at all**. So, if most of the content you are producing is in text format, how many people are you not reaching? If the numbers above are correct I would guess you are missing more than you would like to. The best workaround for this pandemic of illiteracy is to produce content in a format that everyone will understand.

When I say "APPLE" what comes to mind? A juicy fruit, that comes in red, green, and yellowish-green varieties? Or, how about a company that changed the way we live our daily lives? Which one did you choose? Now, what if I said "APPLE" while holding an image of an over-priced iPhone 6? Would that make things a bit more clear?

The exercise above helped me prove a point that otherwise wouldn't have been believed by many readers. That point is: "Just because you know what you are talking about, doesn't mean that everyone else does." As a marketer, your main objective is to give your product or service context. As shown above, "APPLE" without context has a split meaning and therefore diminishes the value of your content.

Now the question becomes; how do I:

1. Produce content that everyone will understand, and

2. How do I add context to my content?

Have I ever told you that you ask the best questions? Well, you do.

My answer to both of those wonderful questions is make videos. Yes, there are many other marketing channels besides videos, and yes, I typically use what I like to call the "Chop Shop" method for my own personal content. However, videos are the simplest and most direct way to reach customers. Also the "Chop Shop" method has many moving parts, as well as its own chapter. See Chapter 9 (pg. 130) for more information.

Three Video Creation Methods

Contrary to popular belief, videos are relatively inexpensive, quick, and easy to produce. In many cases a two-minute video will take less time to create than a two-page paper, and will typically convey more digestible information to your target audience.

There are many different types of videos you can produce for your content strategy. However, most will fall into these three categories:

- Person on Screen

- Screen Sharing
- Text/Images

Person on Screen: This is what most people think of when they hear video marketing; having one or more people in front of a camera, explaining or doing a task. This form of video marketing is why I feel a large majority of small business owners avoid video marketing. They overcomplicate the process. By thinking about how many actors they have to hire, what type of cameras they will have to buy, how much a professional camera crew will cost, or by not wanting to get on camera themselves, they think themselves out of video marketing.

Person on Screen video marketing, especially for smaller companies and home based business owners, doesn't have to be complicated. With a cell phone camera, decent lighting, and great information you've just made a piece of simple and shareable content.

Screen Sharing: This type of video creation is just what it sounds like. It's when a person is sharing his/her screen while explaining or demonstrating something. This method is preferred by many people because it allows them not to be on camera, but it still gets their message across. This method is oftentimes more helpful when trying to teach someone how to do something technical. Such as, using an online platform or mastery of software like Photoshop or Microsoft PowerPoint.

This too can be relatively inexpensive. There are free screen recording options, most notably Jing and Screencast-O-Matic. However, I will admit I do favor "Camtasia" which is on the higher end of screen recorders and will cost you about $75-$200 depending on your computer platform, and where you buy it from. The reason I use Camtasia is I can record and edit my video all on one platform. Still, if you just want to try this out for the first time, or the budget isn't there yet, the free ones will get the job done. Also, Camtasia and other paid screen recorders often offer free trials.

Text/Images: Also known as animation content creation. Text and/or image video creation is the format I truly love. It covers all of the bases. It looks expensive, it looks intimidating enough to the point where people won't try to copy it, it's more brandable, it's more likely to be shared than the other two, it keeps viewers more engaged, and compared to traditional forms of video creation it's super inexpensive. Conversely, I will openly admit that I am biased and this form of video creation does have its downside. It takes longer to produce and it's more expensive than the other two.

This format has to be paired with a certain level of skill and software mastery. Thankfully you have me, and I have a shortcut for just about everything. That's not to say there won't be a learning curve, because TRUST me there will be, but this with the following information the curve will be smaller.

After Effects Animation Shortcut

For those of you book grazers, **you know who you are**. If you don't wish to go through the process of making an animated video you can have it outsourced. You can read the outsource chapter (Chpt. 12 pg. 179) or go to the reference site we've made for this book. The next few paragraphs are about how to hack the text/images video making process, feel free to skip on to the next section.

Ok non-grazers, here are my secrets. I use a site called Videohive.net. For those of you who are familiar with web design, it's owned by the same company that owns Themeforest. If you go to Videohive.net you will see a section that says "After Effects Project Files." If you just hover over it, a drop down should appear. From that drop down you will most likely be looking for "openers" or "product promos." If you are going to use videos as a primary part of your content strategy I suggest getting an explainer pack. These come with several elements, such as, customizable characters, into slides, outros, sound effects, etc.. These packs can be used over and over again without things looking or feeling stale.

Most of the video templates on this site are easy to customize and come with detailed instructions. Also, in most cases if you are feeling stuck you can easily contact the template creator and they will walk you through how to change something. If video isn't your thing don't force it, reach out to the people that created it and they will usually do your project for you for about $30. Never get to the point where you are drowning in a new area, outsource when you can.

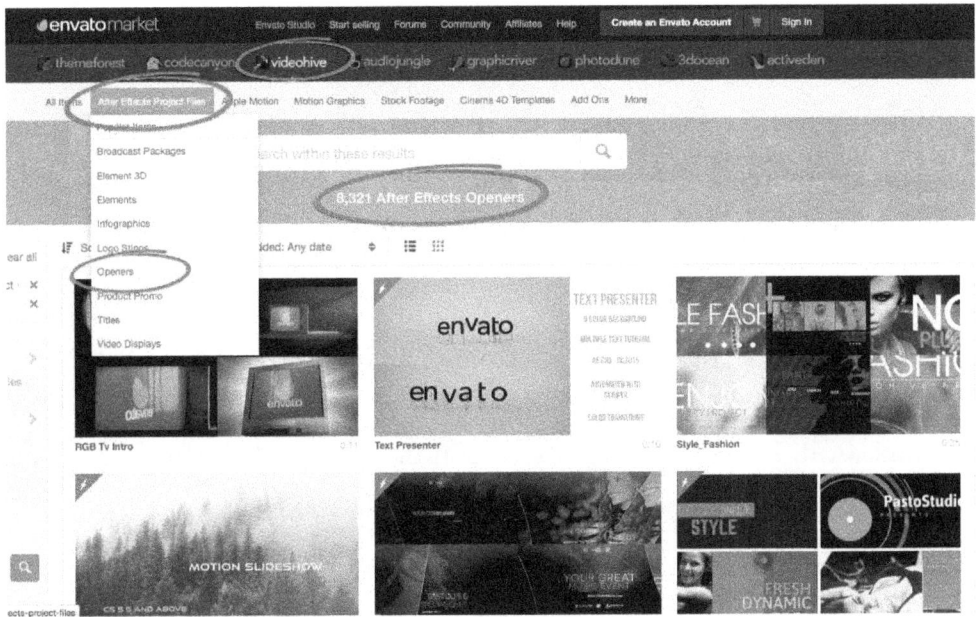

The new After Effects (AE) Software on the cloud will cost about $30/month, however you can buy CS5 copy fairly cheap on eBay or Amazon. The template will run you about $35-$65. Not as bad as traditional marketing, but not free either.

Buyer Beware! A few things to keep in mind:

- Software is best bought from the company that produces it.
- Make sure to check out the copyrights on the products you buy, or want to buy.

101

- Not all templates come with detailed instructions.
- Not all templates come with sound effects/music.
- You may need to turn to YouTube to get some AE basic training.

Once more if all else fails find a video you like, contact the person you bought it from, tell them what you want the video to say and within 72 hours (three days), you have a video that looks like it took months to produce and thousands of dollars to do so. In actuality, if you outsourced, it took you about 30 min. to an hour at max, and about $90-$200.

One last warning, outsourcing always has its risk, so make sure you trust the person. They could run off with your money or worse. Come to think of it, I do know a lovely person that does video marketing. You may have heard of her, short, glasses, co-author of this very book… just a suggestion.

Is the video worth it?

Even if you did one video a month at $500 it would still be worth it. At $6,000 those 12 videos, once properly distributed, could bring in 10 times the investment or more. If you don't believe me, follow the numbers.

- 100 million Internet users will each watch at least 1 video a month.

- 90% of online shoppers prefer to have video to aid retail decisions.
- Videos make people stay engaged two minutes longer, on average.
- 64% of website buyers are more likely to convert.
- Forbes recently reported that 75% of C-level executives watch business related videos at least once a week.
- One week after a visit, 80% of people will remember seeing your video.
  - 46% of that 80% will take some kind of action.
  - 26% will remember the information.
  - 15% will remember the company.
  - 22% will remember the ad.
- Once again, according to Forbes, 59% of senior executives would rather watch a video than read text.

If I went through all of my video statistical information I would have to literally write another 20-page chapter. Just trust me on this one. In most cases having a video is better than not having a video.

Video Distribution Technique

This is a short and sweet section. There's not a lot of detail; everything is pretty self-explanatory. If you are having any problems with videos not loading, the video platforms should have an FAQ or support section.

1. Have a video that looks professional and that is loaded with juicy content.
2. Create five similar but different descriptions for that one video.
   a. Make sure you link to your website/URL/content/item.
   b. Make sure you have a call to action.
3. Come up with keywords (five to ten) for that video.
4. Go to oneload.com. This distribution network will save so much time, and get your video on different video hosting sites.
   a. A free account will do.
   b. Create an account if you don't have one.
   c. Set up your video sharing sites. Start out with five different video platforms.
   d. Make sure YouTube and Vimeo are two of the five
5. Upload the video to the OneLoad platform.
6. Done.

Bonus: What I like to do is stagger the publishing. So instead of one video being published on all five platforms at the same time they come out, they send backlinks to my site at different times during the week.

Example:

I choose five video publishing platforms and my first three are YouTube, Vimeo, Daily Motion, in that order.

- YouTube publishes the video on Monday.
- Vimeo publishes the video on Tuesday.
- Dailymotion publishes the video on Wednesday.
- Bing publishes the video on Thursday.
- Tumblr publishes the video on Friday.

This accomplishes two very important tasks. First, it sends backlinks to my site five days a week. This way high value links look organic and there won't be any flagging. Second, this creates a look of organized consistency for any fans of the individual platforms. Your YouTube people know you post on Monday's and your Vimeo people will always be expecting a video on Tuesday's. The first part is for the robots the second part is for the people, which is the basis of all Internet marketing.

Takeaways

- Video reaches a broader and more diverse audience.

- Video is easier and cheaper than you think!

- You don't have to be in front of the camera to make your video marketing strategy work.

- A well-organized video distribution strategy can help your SEO.

For additional resources and content updates, please visit
ThinkBeyondBuzzwords.com/video-marketing-2

7

The Money's In The List

"To not have an email address is the
digital equivalent of being homeless.
Without it you can't shop online,
bank online or engage with social media."

- Dela Quist

The Email Marketing market will reach $6.5 billion by 2018.

Source: Transparency Market Research (goo.gl/IJpJwZ)

POP QUIZ Which is more popular for staying in touch, email or social media? The answer might surprise you. For as much fan fair as social media gets, email is the perennial favorite globally for staying in touch.

Source: Ipsos (goo.gl/mYwMle)

Few things in the Digital Marketing world are as profitable as an active email list. Yes, email! Not social media, blogging or any other Digital Marketing avenue delivers as much impact to your bottom line revenue as your email list. The reason for this is simple; the person most likely to engage with you online is someone who has already engaged with you in the past. At present, with regard to revenue, email is the undisputed heavyweight champ of the Digital Marketing world… though mobile is poised to unseat it; as email open rates on mobile devices far, FAR exceed that of desktop. As a matter of fact, checking email is the #1 activity performed on a mobile device, not app usage. But this is email's chapter, more on the monster that is mobile in the next chapter.

Marketers rely on email for everything from engagement and lead generation to acquisition and retention. The reasons for having a properly maintained email list extend far beyond mere profit, though. Email marketing programs are typically inexpensive, and in many cases free to create and run. They can be implemented quickly and work in tandem with other marketing efforts such as mobile, mentioned above. But the real reason email has earned its revenue crown is the ability to personalize your message to your customers, track results and easily test and tweak your campaign.

Here comes the law...

But before you get too excited and start blasting off emails as fast as your little fingers can type, we need to have a little talk about the potential pitfalls associated with sloppy email marketing. As previously mentioned in chapter four, the importance of a CAN-SPAM compliant email auto-responder cannot be overstated. Again, the CAN-SPAM Act stands for the:

Control

Against

Non-

Solicited

Pornography

And

Marketing

It's the law that governs commercial email marketing. There can be fines up to $16,000 per email sent. With penalties that hefty, one ill-fated email blast could easily sink your business. However the good news is most, if not all, commercial email auto-responders are CAN-SPAM compliant; so you don't have to worry about that $16,000 per email hammer clobbering you.

As the name implies, an email auto-responder is an email utility that lets you respond automatically (get it... auto-responder) by sending a pre-written email once someone takes a desired action on your site e.g. entering an email address. So if you've ever given up your email address in exchange for a free report or white paper, which was then emailed to you moments later, that was the work of an auto-responder. It's also the typical and preferred manner in which they're used, to build your all important email list!

As with anything else, email auto-responder providers run the gamut from inexpensive to wanting a quart of blood and your first-born child as payment. If you're just starting out we highly recommend MailChimp as the provider of choice. MailChimp is free, that's right, at no cost for the first 2,000 names on your list. And if you can't figure out how to monetize (turn into money) a list of 2,000 people, your auto-responder provider is the least of your worries.

So now that we've gotten you safely out of the clutches of Johnny Law, let's lay the foundation to your email marketing campaign. Given its dominant contribution to bottom line revenue, you could easily fill several books on just email. However, it's beyond the scope of this chapter and this book to do so. In keeping with the theme of the book, this chapter is geared at changing your mindset regarding email marketing. Following is a 10,000 ft. view of an email marketing program. It's not meant to be comprehensive, but should get you well on your way to email marketing done right!

Basic Email Analytics

In order to get the most out of your email marketing efforts we need to start by defining a few terms. While not terribly complicated, email marketing does have it's own language you'd do well to learn. Following are basic email marketing terms.

- Open rate
  - The percentage of subscribers who open your email.
- Bounce rate
  - Hard bounce: an email that cannot be delivered due to a permanent error (e.g. email address is invalid, domain name doesn't exist, etc.).
  - Soft bounce: an email that cannot be delivered due to a temporary error (address is recognized as valid, but the inbox is full or ISP is unavailable).
- Click through rate

- The percentage of subscribers that opened the email and completed the call-to-action (CTA) within.
- Conversion rate
  - The percentage of subscribers who become customers.

Subject Lines

So now that we have a few terms defined, let's go on to the single most important part of your email, the subject line! That's right, hands down the most important part of the email is the subject line. Without it, nothing you write matters because no one will ever see it. Think of your subject line as your digital first impression. And we all know you don't get a second chance to make a first one of those. Email is even less forgiving. Below are some guidelines to follow when crafting that all-important subject line.

Email subject lines should be:

- Compelling
- Concise
- Relevant
- Beneficial to the recipient

Be sure to utilize target audience demographics gleaned from sites like Alexa.com, Quantcast.com, etc. Review both print and online newspaper headlines for ideas e.g. Yahoo News, TMZ, etc.

Email Creative

Congratulations! You got past the hard part of getting your prospective customers to open your email. Believe it or not 80% of the work is done. Woo Hoo!!! But this is no time to rest on your laurels… (what are laurels anyway?) Let's not waste all that hard work you put into getting your subscribers this far. Now that they're here, you need to focus on the desired action you want them to take.

- Create Brand Impact
  - When subscribers open your email they should immediately recognize your brand and feel all the positive emotions your brand elicits. Use a style guide for consistency with your website, logo etc.
- Make No Assumptions
  - You can't assume your subscribers will read every single line of your email. Front-load it with the important information. Also, it's not a good idea to reference other ad campaigns, unless the email is part of a series. If you

reference something they haven't seen yet they'll have no idea what you're talking about!

- Drive the Purchase
  - ALWAYS ask for the sale… but not in an obnoxious way like using all caps. Use tact of course, but at the same time don't be shy with your call-to-action (CTA). **A marketing email with no CTA is just a note.**
- Create Transactional/Service Messages (Auto-Responders)
  - We covered this above, when you're actually pre-writing these messages a great thing to keep in mind is that the subscriber is actually expecting this email, or else they wouldn't have given you their email address in the first place. This is the perfect time to cross-promote other products, include coupons, etc.
- Add Viral Elements
  - Share, share, SHARE!!! There is no better brand evangelist than a satisfied customer. Therefore, we want to make it as easy as possible for our subscribers to share our message. Make sure you include a "Forward to a friend" link in your message. And of course, every email should have the standard social media share buttons on the bottom.

Testing your email

"Every email is a customer survey of your target market, by testing they vote on what resonates best with them."

~ Kath Pay

Don't forget one of the most valuable aspects of email marketing, testing! Multivariate or A/B split testing is when you test two different versions of one section of your email. It works best if you only test one section at a time so you can pinpoint which version is performing better. So test two different versions of the subject line, but leave the ad copy alone. Test the ad copy, but leave the subject line alone, etc.

Constant Contact is a great resource for more information on A/B split testing. When testing your emails always be sure to do the following:

- Add all of your own personal email addresses to the test list.
- Check all of your personal email accounts for deliverability.
- Open your email.
- Click around
  - Are the images displayed properly?
  - Are the links clickable?
  - Do the links lead the subscriber to the right landing page?
  - Are there any spelling errors?

115

Check your email analytics for open rate and clicks to determine your winner. And there you have it! A solid foundation on which to further your knowledge on email marketing.

Takeaways

- The Money's In The List!
- Stay CAN-SPAM Compliant.
- Get A Good Auto-Responder.
- Test, Test, Test!

End of Chapter Resources

Again, this chapter was not meant to be exhaustive in nature, but rather give you a working knowledge of the importance of email marketing to the bottom line of your business. Below, you'll find some additional resources for further study.

- Marketing Profs, *Email Open and Click Rates: Benchmarks Trends* (goo.gl/4s7nnT).
- Mail Chimp, *Email Marketing Benchmarks* (goo.gl/Gi0ejg).

- Email Stat Center: The Leading Authority on Email Marketing Metrics (goo.gl/sWB4dw).
- Marketo, *The New Metrics for Email Marketing* (goo.gl/WmFEOP).
- CAN-SPAM Act: A Compliance Guide for Business (goo.gl/v6da6Z).

For additional resources and content updates, please visit ThinkBeyondBuzzwords.com/email-marketing

8

Go Mobile or Die

"Strategies that don't perform well
on mobile won't perform well at all!"

-Greg Hickman,
Mobile Marketing Engine

I graduated Salutatorian from Full Sail University's Internet Marketing Bachelor's of Science program on Friday March 6th, 2015. I relocated from Dayton, OH to Atlanta, GA the very next day. Now that I was all graduated I had six months to find Sallie Mae's money. The job market in Atlanta, GA is much, MUCH stronger than that of Dayton, OH so there is where I went.

Not one month later, on April 1st I started work as a Jr. Digital Sales Analyst at MoonConfidence Bank corporate headquarters in Downtown Atlanta. MoonConfidence (not the real name because I don't want to be sued) is one of the largest and most prestigious regional banks in the Southeast. I was very honored and brimming with pride to have landed that gig straight out of college.

Well, the April Fool's joke was on me when a mere 27 days later I was unceremoniously fired. The reason they gave was "you're just not a good fit." And in all honesty I really wasn't! I'd have done much better on their corporate marketing team, not as an analyst on the sales team. But shed no tears on my behalf, because a mere three weeks later I started another job that paid $2/hr more, or $4,000 more a year! So all MoonConfidence did by dropping me like a bad habit was give me a three week vacation and a $4,000 a year raise. Thanks!

But before MoonConfidence kicked me to the curb, I was almost exclusively tasked with helping prepare for April 21st when Google announced they would start using mobile friendliness as a ranking signal in their search algorithm. In other words, if your website isn't mobile friendly, Google's going to start demoting your listing in the search engine results page or SERP. This is a big, BIG deal, and MoonConfidence was making absolutely certain they were prepared for that day.

WARNING: Bad Joke Alert Where's the best place to hide a dead body? On page two of Google, no one will ever find it there! Now feel free to be dismissive of whatever I say, but please know that one of the largest regional banks in the Southeast would not put crazy overtime into preparing for something if it wasn't absolutely essential. If you believe nothing else, you can believe that.

So why was the April 21st algorithm update, playfully dubbed Mobilegeddon, so darn important? There are several reasons…

1. Google NEVER announces an algorithm update in advance.

Reiterating from chapter two; PPC is easy while SEO is hard. This is because at its core SEO is reverse engineering. This level of difficulty is further compounded by that fact that Google typically comes clean about a major algorithm update about a month AFTER they've done it, not before. It was unprecedented for Google to give a couple months' heads up on an impending algorithm update. That just speaks to the importance of this update.

2. Mobile is officially here!

During the summer of 2015 worldwide Google searches performed on mobile devices surpassed the number of searches done on desktop for the first time in history. In the Digital Marketing community we've been talking for years about how "mobile is coming." Well, as of 2015 mobile is officially here!

3. Google owns Android – Android Owns Mobile.

On smartphones the operating system is the software that powers the device. The major operating systems are Google's Android, Apple's iOS and to a lesser extent Research In Motion's Blackberry. Not unlike their stranglehold on the search market, Google's Android has about 70% market share of smartphone operating systems. So strategically it makes a lot of sense for them to push the envelope with mobile and further fortify their position.

Need Further Convincing?

I know what you're thinking, that's all well and good, but is mobile for me? The quote at the beginning of the chapter is from a guy named Greg Hickman. Previously he was the head of mobile marketing for Cabela's (an outdoor sporting goods retailer similar to Bass Pro Shop), but now has his own mobile marketing firm, Mobile Marketing Engine.

He also hosted the *Mobile Friendly* podcast of which I was an avid listener. Unfortunately, the podcast was on hiatus as of this writing.

For months on the podcast Greg had been referencing a conversation he had with a successful business owner who told him businesses only grow three ways, regardless of strategy or tactic:

- Get new customers.
- Get existing customers to spend more (order size).
- Get existing customers to spend more often (frequency).

Of the three, getting new customers is by far the most difficult and the most expensive. Yet this is where most small business owners focus their attention. But as know from Chapter 7 on email, the person most likely to buy from you is someone who had bought from you before.

While there are arguably better ways of accomplishing the first outcome listed above, mobile is AMAZING at customer engagement (outcomes two and three). But don't just take my word for it, here are some compelling facts as to why mobile is absolutely essential for business going forward.

Consumers are mobile

- In 2013, 60% made mobile purchases at least once a month (https://goo.gl/5tJr4x).

- 65% of US smartphone users check their phones within 15 minutes of waking up. 64% check their phones within 15 minutes of going to bed (https://goo.gl/Lw06vc).

- By 2018, U.S. mobile retail revenues are expected to amount to $130.12 billion, up from $56.67 billion in 2014 (http://goo.gl/L31BCr).

- Mobile digital media time in the US is significantly higher at 51%, compared to desktop at 42% (https://goo.gl/Lw06vc).

- 67% have used their smartphones every day in the past seven days (https://goo.gl/5tJr4x).

- 83% don't leave home without their device (https://goo.gl/5tJr4x).

- 96% of smartphone use is at home; 84% on the go; 83% in a store (https://goo.gl/5tJr4x).

Mobile Search

- 61% search on their smartphones every day (https://goo.gl/5tJr4x).

- Research that starts on mobile 40% then purchase online via computer, 38% then purchase offline in-store (https://goo.gl/5tJr4x).

- 56% have performed a mobile search after seeing an ad (https://goo.gl/5tJr4x).

- Mentioning a location in mobile ads and search results can increase click-through rates up to 200% (http://goo.gl/n6YlZs).

- 94% of smartphone users look for local information on their phone; 84% take action as a result (https://goo.gl/5tJr4x).

- 77% of mobile users have researched a product or service on their mobile device; 46% of smartphone users have made a purchase on their phone (https://goo.gl/5tJr4x).

Mobile Website Optimization

- 74% of consumers will wait five seconds for a web page to load on their mobile device before abandoning the site (http://goo.gl/SxSSdQ).

- 46% of consumers are unlikely to return to a mobile site if it didn't work properly during their last visit (http://goo.gl/SxSSdQ).

- 71% of mobile browsers expect web pages to load almost as quickly or faster as web pages on their desktop computers (http://goo.gl/SxSSdQ).

SMS Mobile Marketing

- Over 90% of text messages are read three within minutes of receipt (http://goo.gl/SxSSdQ).

- SMS alone contributed 33.5 percent of mobile data revenues worldwide in 2015, to retain its position as the single biggest contributor. In 2015, in North America SMS still generated 30.1 percent of mobile data revenues (https://goo.gl/Lw06vc).

Mobile Social Media

- 83% visit social networks; 56% visit at least once a day (https://goo.gl/5tJr4x).

- 78% of Facebook's users are mobile-only (https://goo.gl/Lw06vc).

- 36% would rather give up TV than their smartphone (https://goo.gl/5tJr4x).

Mobile Email

- If all U.S. mobile Internet time were condensed into an hour, 25 minutes of it would be spent on email (http://goo.gl/ICSYaV).

- 64% of decision makers read their email via mobile devices (https://goo.gl/Lw06vc).

Expertise in Mobile Has Never Been More Valuable

Michael J. Becker is a former managing director of the Mobile Marketing Association (MMA). In his role with the MMA, he grew the industry so that all businesses and all players within the mobile ecosystem continue to succeed and innovate. He's a wealth of knowledge about the unique intersection between mobile and traditional marketing and how mobile is engaging consumers in unique and effective ways.

Mr. Becker recently partnered with Paul Barney to found mobile marketing agency mCordis. *Cordis* is Latin for "of the heart" and they want to put mobile at the heart of marketing. It is also a name that reflects their passions.

http://www.mcordis.com/about/mcordis-management-team

I became aware of Mr. Becker through his Mobile Marketing Fundamentals course on Lynda.com (recently acquired by LinkedIn.com). In the course, Mr. Becker lays out the different players in the Mobile Marketing spaces as:

- Consumers
- Marketers
- Sellers
- Enablers
- Associates

I'll let you watch the course for the definition and context of these players so as not to steal Mr. Becker's thunder... or violate Lynda.com's copyright. But what I want you to take away from this is how Mr. Becker sums it up:

> "See, I told you that the market was complex. In fact, it's much like a rain forest with many tiered layers of life. Every player, like in the rain forest is fighting for survival and reward."

I reached out to Michael J. Becker prior to the Mobilegeddon announcement for his take on mobile and the industry as a whole. However, this interview takes on new significance in the wake of Mobilegeddon. This interview is almost 45 minutes long and over 60 pages typed, so it wasn't appropriate to transcribe it all in this chapter. You can find it on YouTube at the link below.

Special thanks to Mr. Becker for supplying us with magnificently mobile *Killer Bees – Killer Content*:

Full Video Interview: https://goo.gl/rEw2Xa

Takeaways

- Mobile isn't coming; it's here!

- It's a really, really big deal.

- Use mobile to grow your business.

- NOTHING engages like mobile!

- Mobile expertise has never been more valuable.

For additional resources and content updates, please visit
ThinkBeyondBuzzwords.com/mobile

9

The "Chop Shop" Method

Content Creation & Distribution Made Easy

*"If you love your life, don't waste time.
For time is what life is made out of."*

-Bruce Lee

Most of the people reading this book will know content is king. If you just so happen to be in the minority, and not know that, just take my word for it. If you still find yourself being a nonbeliever, there is a book with that very title to prove my point. With that being said, if you have ever tried to create content on a consistently, steady basis you've probably noticed how hard it can be.

Not only do you have to find something to talk about, you also have to find time to create that content, then figure out what format to put it in, then when to post it, and so on and so forth. I have a quick and easy solution for this I like to call the "Chop Shop" method.

For those of you who aren't from the hood, or who haven't watched urban crime movies lately, a chop shop is a place where a vehicle, usually stolen, is disassembled and its parts are refurbished for profit.

"What does that have to do with online content, Michelle?"

Follow me for a moment here. If you treat your content like thieves treat a chop shop car, you will: create more content, more backlinks, and more social buzz. I'm going to give you an example and you'll see what I'm talking about.

I make a video about social media Ads. From that video I create a blog post. From that same video, I extract the sound to create an audio file. Using the information from the video I then create (or outsource) an infographic or image of some sort. So far I have four unique pieces of content from one idea, but let's go a bit further.

Distribution Strategy:

Sunday:

- Create a Video. At the end of the video ask for questions and feedback. Let the audience know that within the week you will create another video answering their questions and concerns.
- Distribute that video using video distribution services like Oneload.com

Monday:

- Create a blog post from the information in the video. A very simple shortcut for this is to exact the audio (explained in the Tuesday section below) and upload the mp3 file to a program like Dragon Dictation, which is a speech to text software. This makes a transcription of the video, leaving you with just the text.
- Add the video to the blog post as well.

Tuesday:

- Extract the sound from the video and upload the mp3 to iTunes and Soundcloud.com.

132

- o There are many Firefox and Chrome plugins that will allow you to do this. Just search in the appropriate plugin resources spots for your browser. I use *YouTube Video and Audio Downloader* for Firefox.

- Create a short Google+ & Facebook post using your content.
  - o Include a simple, catchy headline and a link to your blog.

Wednesday:

- Create an infographic, or an image of some kind, that expresses the information presented in the video. If you're not the best with photoshop you can use templates. There are many businesses out there that will make it for you. Piktochart.com is a service you can use that has drag and drop features to get your graphic done quickly.
- Upload that graphic to Instagram and Pinterest with a rich description linking back to the blog post.

Thursday:

- Send out a tweet.
  - o Use a catchy intro.

133

- o If you have space, use terms like "live video response." Just let them know that if they have questions you will answer them.
- Send an e-mail out to your list using the same tips for Twitter above.

Friday:

- Create another video answering the questions and concerns from the video created on Sunday. If you don't have a very big following, or if no one responds to your video, add more information to the content that you have already.
  - o Preferably this would be a "Hangout On Air" or a recorded live webinar. Allow your fans to interact with you. Most of them won't bite...most of them.

Saturday:

- Create a SlideShare (A PowerPoint or Keynote presentation uploaded to a platform called SlideShare) using the information in the original video, and the follow up video you made on Friday.

From ONE video you have created

1. A blog post
2. A Soundcloud audio
3. An Itunes/Podcast audio

4. A Facebook Post

5. A Google+ Post

6. An Instagram Post

7. A Pinterest Post

8. A solid, info packed tweet

9. Another Video

10. A SlideShare file

Not too shabby if I do say so myself. Not only did you just create ten pieces of content, you've created ten plus organic, social-oriented, backlinks to your company site, branding site, etc.

Don't forget to link all newly created content to a branding terminal that you own, like your blog, business website, or personal branding site. If you don't have any of these things, link to a place where you want people to find you, like Google+.

Takeaway

- Making content doesn't have to be hard.

- One piece of content can be broken down into multiple pieces of content.

- A good distribution strategy can stretch content even further.

For additional resources and content updates, please visit
ThinkBeyondBuzzwords.com/content-creation

10

The Monetary Magic of Numbers

"When you have mastered numbers,
you will in fact no longer be reading numbers,
any more than you read words
when reading books.
You will be reading meanings."

—W. E. B. Du Bois

Analytics according to the *Scholarly Dictionary of Michelle A. Bassett* is the tracking, formatting, and understanding of data. Without analytics you, as a marketer or small business owner, cannot make educated decisions. Without data and the understanding of that data you are just guessing, and worse than that you are leaving money on the table. A prime example of this is my friend "Kevin."

Kevin has an ecommerce site. He sells t-shirts with cute little nerdy sayings on them, like Dr. Who quotes and popular memes he'd find throughout the cosmos of the Internet. Kevin did well for himself. He had his sales data and knew what items he sold more of, but he didn't really know where his sales were coming from. He did Facebook Ads, Google Adwords, and Outbrain banner ads. In total, his monthly ad spend was about $3,000 and his monthly revenue was about $4,500 a month. From the outside looking in, Kev wasn't doing all that bad; but when you have a friend like me… I'm going to tell you about yourself.

I didn't have a problem with his ROI; I had a problem with his lack of data.

If I'm losing you in the conversation right now here's a spoiler alert: Once I was done with his site, that $3,000 when down to $2,800 and that $4,500 went up to $5,159. That's the power of understanding data! So, hold tight and stick with the story.

Once more it wasn't a ROI issue, I was saddened that he didn't have a clue on how to replicate his success or even grow it. All he knew was that he used those ad platforms mentioned above, and that he sold roughly 155 shirts a month. He didn't know what ad platform worked best, he didn't know what people were doing once they got to the site, he had no way of getting back in front of those people and he didn't know why his number one selling T-shirt was his number one selling T-shirt.

"Who cares why Michelle?" Do you remember that spoiler above? That's why everyone, especially someone who runs a small business, should care.

In the next sections I'm going to go over a few higher-level analytics. If you don't get it the first time don't worry, just go back and read the section again. If you still don't understand something, please use the resource website to get a deeper understanding of how web analytics can help your business grow.

Getting Started

1. The very first thing to start the analytics process is a Google Analytics (GA) account. The account is free, and the sign up is easy.

For sign up and installation instructions please visit the resource area at: www.ThinkBeyondBuzzWords.com/Analytics.

If you are already using an analytic service besides Google, or if you just want to use a different service, that's fine. The information may not be in the same location as I'll be describing below for Google, but what

I've found is that the terms I'm going to use in this chapter are pretty much standard across platforms.

2. The next thing you want to do is link your analytic service to your merchant services. If you are using Google, this means linking your **Adwords Account,** and for some of you your **AdSense Account,** to your Google Analytics Account. Also make sure that you set up your conversion goals.

Adwords is a PPC platform where you pay for clicks or impressions; AdSense is a PPC platform where you get paid for clicks or impressions.

3. Set conversion goals and identify your **KPI**.

Key Performance Indicator(s) or KPI is a business metric used to evaluate factors that are critical to the performance of the campaign. Each campaign is unique and each may have a different set of KPIs. To learn more about KPIs and how to choose the right one for you, please visit the chapter resource URL.

4. Next, you want to drive traffic to your website or landing page for approximately 30-90 days. Why so long? The more data you have the better, especially if you have less than 1,000 visitors a month. Waiting for

90 days may seem like a long time, but if you are taking massive action and using the other principles in this book, time will fly by. No worries. With that being said, if you have 5,000 visitors on average a month after the first 30 days of data collection, then by all means go to the next section and start tweaking.

Understand Your Numbers

Yay! You've made it to the tweaking phase! This is my favorite phase in Digital Marketing. This is where the magic happens and the money is made.

And The Winner Is: Know Which Advertising Platform Works Best.

When you open up your Google Analytics you'll most likely be on your Overview tab. For this area of understanding we are going to focus on the tab called Acquisition.

Inside of Acquisition, click on overview, you should see something that looks like this:

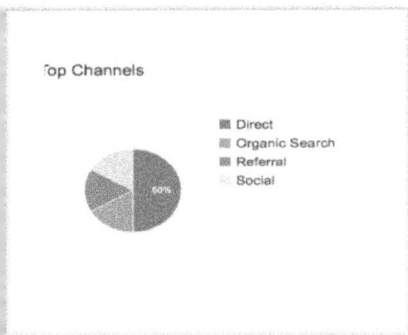

Top Channels

- Direct
- Organic Search
- Referral
- Social

Next to that pie chart there will be session information as well as conversion information. If you did not set up your conversion information when you started your tracking, this line chart will have 0's across the board. For this book, we are only going to focus on the "Top Channels." Again, if you would like more detailed information please use the free resource area we've provided.

As you can see the majority of my traffic for this URL is **direct**. Meaning someone had the exact URL and typed it into their browser. My **Organic**, **Referral**, and **Social** are about 16% a piece. Organic means the user went to a search engine, like Google or Bing, typed words into the search bar and clicked on my website. Referral means another website (typically paid) provided a backlink (a link to my website) and that's how that user wound up on my site. Social means they "organically" found me through a social media platform, like Facebook, LinkedIn, or Twitter. I put organically in quotes because in many cases the social traffic is generated through a paid social media campaign, but sometimes it's not.

To figure out what platform is providing the most visitors click on the item named "Referral." In that area you will see a section of all of the websites that sent traffic to you. The one with the highest amount sessions and the highest percentage of Goal Conversion rates is the winner.

"Is it really that simple?" …Well … no. There are a number of factors that you have to take into account. Did you spend the same amount of money on each platform? Did you run the same ad with the same ad copy on each platform? So on and so forth. But, will this metric do for now?…yes.

Another, more foolproof way of finding out which ad platform is right for you is to use the analytics tools given to you by the ad platform you are using, in conjunction with the analytics from your website.

That may seem really brief to the analytic heavy hitters, but for the majority of the readers that is exactly the right amount of information you will need to effectively run and understand analytics for your small businesses. Once more, the resources site will have more in-depth tips and tricks.

Whatcha Doin'?

If you want to know what your traffic is doing on your site, you are going to have to add two weapons to your analytics arsenal. The first is called a heat map and the second is the behavior flow chart inside of Google Analytics.

For heat maps I thought it would be best to start off with an image. I know the print is in black and white and it may be hard to see. Please use the resources web page to see the image in full color.

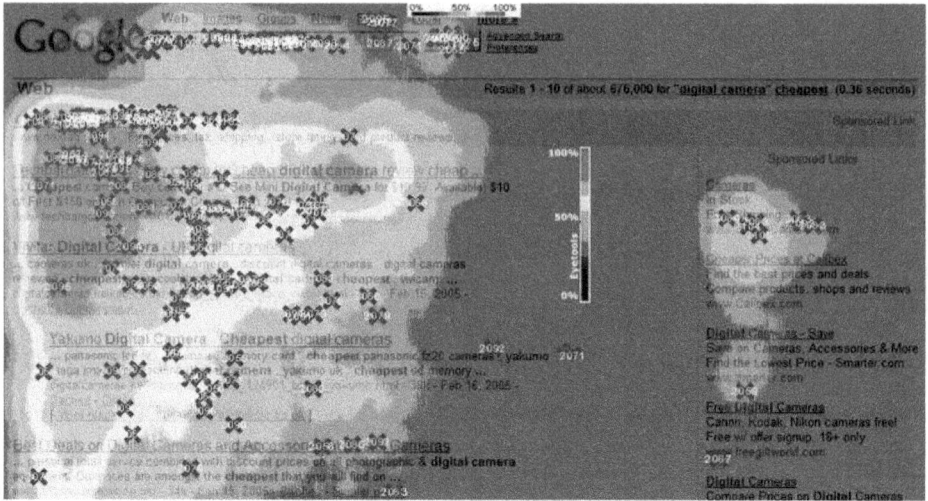

To see in full color go to resource website. ThinkBeyondBuzzwords.com/analytics

Heat maps are a pretty simple concept to get down. If you think about the colors like the ones for the weather forecast, you'll be good to go. Cold places are icy blue like Alaska. I'm sure that's a nice state and all, but I haven't heard too many people say, "You know what, Michelle? This year I'm going to save up to vacation in Alaska this winter." Whereas people say, "This year I'm going to save up to vacation in Florida this winter, where it's hot, and shows up red in my daily weather forecast." Ok, maybe not that last part, but you get the picture.

The easiest way to get heat map access on your site if you are using WordPress is to search for "heat map plugin.". A whole host of options will appear. If you are not using WordPress, and aren't fluent in CSS or HTML I'd suggest using a company like Crazyegg. They will help you step-by-step with your heat map.

144

Now the justification for the heat map is to see where most of your visitors are clicking. The most powerful way to use this data is to see what area is getting the most attention and then rearranging information, images, products or services to encourage your visitors to click on another page, to buy a product, to friend you on social networks, so on and so forth.

That was the first way, again fairly easy to understand once you get it installed and going. The second way is a little more complex, but I guarantee you will enjoy me embarrassing myself, as I spill my master analytical secrets.

Behavioral Flowcharts

Inside of Google Analytics go to the Behavior tab (don't click the Audience tab first and then the Behavior tab). When you click on that, items will appear in a drop down like fashion. One of those items will be named "Behavior Flow." If you click on that you will be able to see exactly where visitors are going on your site. See image below.

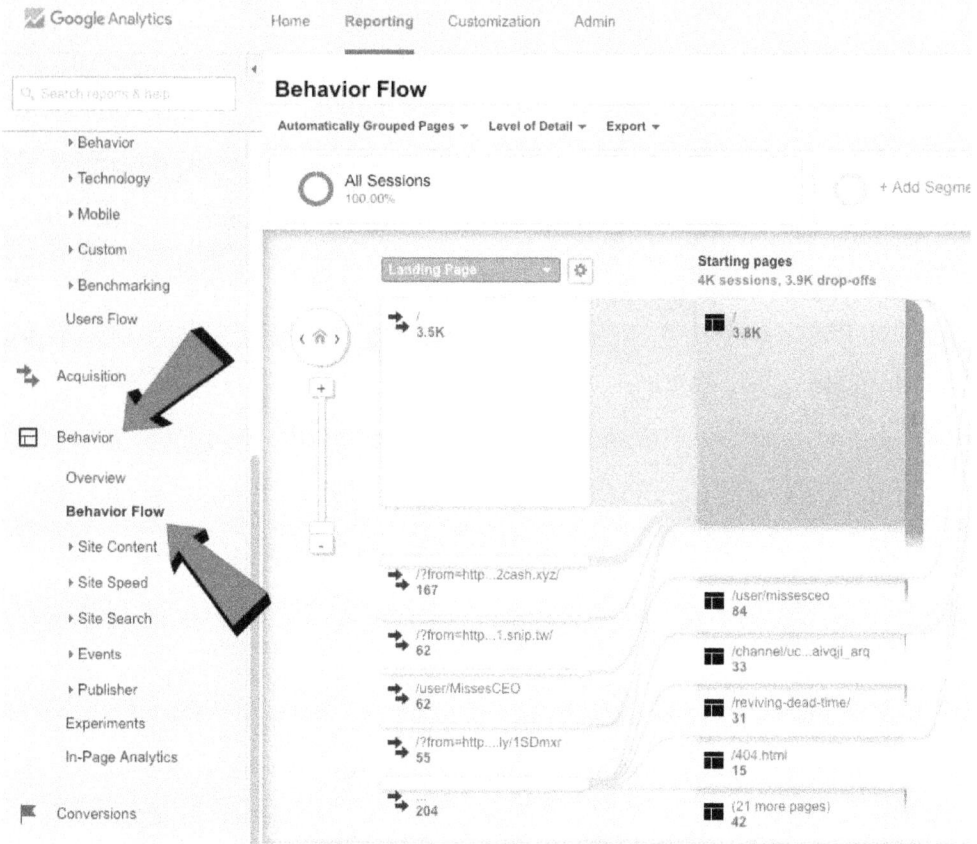

Behavior Flow

Automatically Grouped Pages ▾   Level of Detail ▾   Export ▾

All Sessions
100.00%   + Add Segme

Landing Page ⚙   Starting pages
4K sessions, 3.9K drop-offs

/ 3.5K   / 3.8K

/?from=http...2cash.xyz/ 167   /user/missesceo 84

/?from=http...1.snip.tw/ 62   /channel/uc...aivqji_arq 33

/user/MissesCEO 62   /reviving-dead-time/ 31

/?from=http...ly/1SDmxr 55   /404.html 15

204   (21 more pages) 42

The green areas are the visitors. The red is where they left, or "dropped off." The light blue pathways show where the traffic went, if they didn't drop off. I like to think of the light blue lines as the invisible highway that my traffic follows.

I'm a firm believer that data is just a bunch of numbers, jumbled up, making noise, *if* you don't know what to do with them. So, what do all of those colors and numbers mean? How do you turn that wailing banshee sound into the harmonious melody of a church choir on Sunday morning?

146

You have to follow the traffic flow, like a treasure map.

I typically create a character. This avatar of sorts can be anyone, from any background, with any name, and I trace their steps like I'm a detective on *CSI, Law & Order* or *Cold Case*. It sounds absolutely insane, but it will make the job 20 times more fun, trust me.

I wouldn't be me, if I didn't totally embarrass myself and give you an example, so here goes nothing. Use the image below to see if you can follow the story of Tammy.

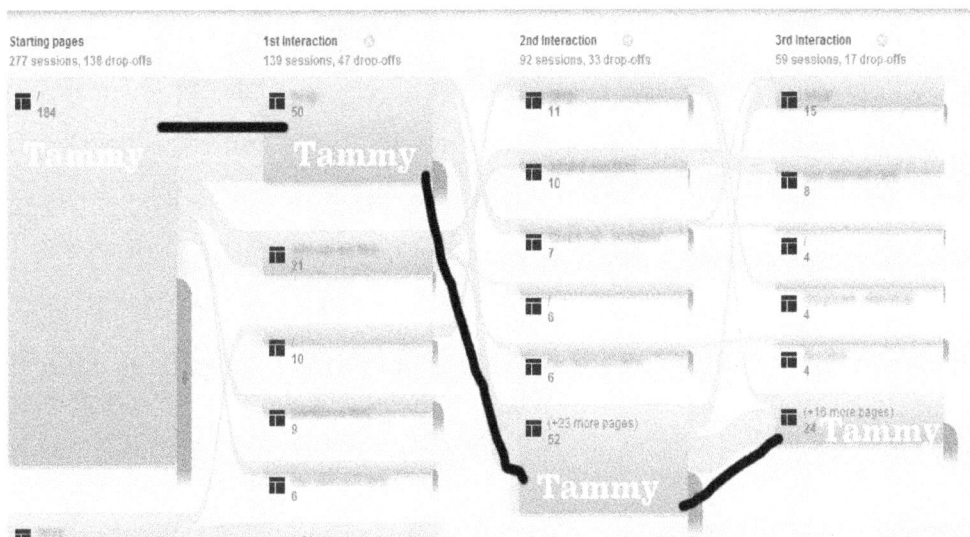

Tammy, a 31-year-old, computer engineer, 3rd of 5 children and expectant mother herself comes to my website via a Google+ post. Curious about an article on the constraints of social reach in the coming years, she clicks on it, moving to the 1st interaction. Seeing another juicily titled article, she then clicks on that title, moving her to the 2nd interaction.

While on that page Tammy sees my ad for my latest book. She has a great experience reading my content so far, and thinks that getting more information about the book won't hurt so she clicks once more, moving her to the 3rd interaction slot. But then tragedy strikes! Tammy's smart phone dies and she falls off into the abyss of the Internet, never getting to experience the joy of reading my skillfully crafted, educational, and life changing material. Hey I didn't say the story had to have a happy ending, I just said that it had to be a story.

That was a silly example, but I made the numbers fun. I made them tell a story, and most importantly, I got to track the path of my real life traffic.

The Tammy story ended because of something I made up, something I can't prove, therefore it isn't true; but what if I could get real data on the drop off visitors? How valuable would that be?

What if on the 2nd interaction Tammy was on my book page learning more about the content, when she made up her mind to buy the book, and moved on to the 3rd interaction. There she clicks the buy button and the shopping cart page doesn't load and she then becomes a drop off. You wouldn't have known this if you weren't following the story and clicking along with Tammy, following her trail around your site. The only way you will know that certain things aren't working is to follow the map.

You may be surprised about the things that aren't working on your site. I was working on this one case where the buy button on every page worked except this one page. Sadly for the guy that owned the site, it was the main place where most of his traffic was directed.

There is so much more information I would like to share about the behavior flow charts, especially as a behavior analyst, but this is only one book, with so many pages, and I have so many other things to share with you. Just keep in mind that you can click and drill down into the different parts of the chart. Click around and build a more detailed picture, and a more interesting story. If you have the urge, send me a screenshot and tell me your traffic story. My contact information is at the end of the book.

Meet Back Up with Your Customers

Have you ever been minding your own business, hanging out on the Internet and bam! All of a sudden you're hit with ads of things that you were looking at on Amazon, eBay, or another website. When this first happened to me a few years back I was pretty freaked out!

I was online, window shopping as usual, being a proud contributor to eBay's high cart abandonment rate. When I clicked open a new tab and logged onto my Facebook there it was. The very same item I was just looking at on eBay, but on my Facebook!

As a self-proclaimed paranoid conspiracy theorist, I knew in my heart of hearts that it had to be the NSA. Later, I found out that my experience was linked to something called Remarketing.

Remarketing, also known as Retargeting, is one of my favorite marketing strategies to date. First of all it's cheaper, second it's more "targeted," and third, of all the ways to invest your marketing dollars online, it has the highest ROI (return on investment).

If this has never happened to you, try it now. Go on Amazon.com and put something in your shopping cart. Wait about five minutes then go on a popular blog or log into one of your social media accounts. It's a book...I'll wait.

Did you do it?!? Freaky, right?

If you wish to hold onto your innocence a little while longer DO NOT READ the next paragraph. If you wish to make more sales online, spending less money, this is how Remarketing happens.

You've already been exposed to the "front end" of Remarketing, here's the backend of the beast. The owner or webmaster of the site in question places a pixel code on his or her website. This code is provided by whatever ad network they wish to use. The most popular networks used for Remarketing are Google Adwords and Facebook Ads. There are other networks and most have their own Retargeting/Remarketing pixel code.

This code places a cookie on your visitor's web browser and tracks them through the Internet. Whenever that visitor hits a site that supports the ad network associated with the cookie, the webmaster's ad will trigger.

With Remarketing the Cost Per Click (CPC) is much lower, and the targeting is much higher, especially for users that placed items in shopping carts. With these visitors you already know that they were interested and exactly what they wanted to buy.

If the shear power of this hasn't sunk in yet, apply it to your business.

Imagine that you've spent money driving traffic to your website, and you have 100 visitors and only two buy something for $20 a piece. The other 98 visitors do their own thing. Some click around the website for a bit, others just leave, never to be heard from again.

Now imagine that you've placed a Remarketing pixel on your landing page. You've spent money driving traffic to your website, and you have 100 visitors and only two buy something for $20 a piece. The other 98 visitors do their own thing. Some click around the website for a bit, others just leave. Over the next seven to 30 days those 98 visitors see your product or service two to three times a day. By day three, four people come back and one buys. At day seven, five more people come back and two buy. At day ten, three people got a paycheck so they come back and buy. Each transaction is $20.

So, instead of making that measly $40 from the first scenario, you've now made $40 on day one, $20 on day three, $40 on day seven and $60 on day ten, for a grand total of $160. That's four times the money and roughly the same budget. If that doesn't get you going I don't know what will!

Know Why Your Best Seller Sells then Sell More

Using the information from behavior analytics and the heat maps you can see what positions and copy on your site is driving the most clicks. For a lot of websites I've worked on, the areas with the most clicks were usually the revolving banner, content above the fold, and buttons that have strong calls to action. However, your website may have totally different results based off of the types of visitors to your site. So, make sure you test your own site.

Once you have the data, have fun! Test out different page copy, different images, different colors, or a different site layout. Go crazy with it! I know it's hard to keep track of things when you have to go to the bank to deposit your barrel of money, but don't forget to test, test, test! The results may surprise you. The smallest things can make all of the difference.

Thus far you have learned how to figure out:

- Which platform works best for your website.
- What people are doing when they come to your website.
- How to get back in front of those people through marketing you're already doing; and
- How a little site manipulation can change what products sell the most.

Now it's time to revisit my good ole friend "Kevin" and his t-shirt company. This is exactly what I did.

First I set up his accounts. He already had a Google Analytics account and some tracking codes already installed, so that was one less thing I had to do. I did however have to install a heat map plugin and create remarketing pixels for Facebook and Google Adwords.

Secondly, I figured out what platform worked the best for him. In his case, Facebook worked best. With that information I took money from Adwords and Outbrain and beefed up the Facebook campaigns. With the money saved from under-performing campaigns, I also created a remarketing campaign in Adwords.

Thirdly, I used the heat map and behavior flow chart to manipulate and **split test** the positions of products, and web copy to figure out the best combination for higher sells. I also used that data to fill in any missing gaps in my sales funnels.

<Related side note> I figured out that the people really liked the flat images of the shirts versus the ones shown on real people. It's counter intuitive, but that is what his audience showed a preference to. *</Related side note>*

Lastly, after 60 days of tweaking ... and no payment, I wrote him up a 30-day maintenance plan. The plan included hypothetical, yet likely, scenarios and what to do in those instances.

So, yes that was fairly simple. Yes, he went from spending $3,000 to $2,800. Yes, his revenue increased roughly $659 ($4,500 to $5,159). Lastly, yes, you can have the same success for your business as he did with his. Let me say it again, "This information and data collection process is _not_ just for someone selling t-shirts!" Any business that generates sales online can use these tools to lower advertising costs while improving overall sales. All you have to do is understand the numbers. Read them like you read a bedtime story to a small child. Make that data come to life, and follow the treasure map to the land of successful businesses and abundance for all.

Now that you have a nice overview of analytics, and can see what the possibility of knowing the numbers can do for you, move on to the next section and get a Killer Bee perspective from Mike King.

Web Analytics with Mike King of iPullRank

While many associate the name Michael King with SEO, his career and contributions to the Digital Marketing industry at large are far greater. As the founder of iPullRank in New York City, Mike King (aka @iPullRank on Twitter) leads teams covering consumer insights, content & social strategy, SEO and marketing automation. In the past, he's worked at mid-tier search firm Enterprise, and led brands such as SAP, HSBC, SanDisk and Wharton among others to digital success.

With previous experience as a Marketing Director, Developer and Tactical SEO at multi-national agencies such as Publicis Modem and Razorfish working for brands like Ralph Lauren, Johnson & Johnson, LG and Citibank; Mike's breadth and depth of experience continues to fuel game changing insights.

Mike King is a sought-after speaker on the Digital Marketing conference circuit, a frequent blogger for Inbound Marketing software company Moz and a published author that loves to share his insights on how to do better marketing.

http://ipullrank.com/about/

I asked Mike for his unique take on analytics and he was gracious enough to bless us with this chapter's *Killer Bees – Killer Content*.

155

Interview Video Source: https://goo.gl/7gd7gV

Transcription:

Temitayo Osinubi = TO   **Mike King = MK**

TO: Alright thanks so much for joining me. My name is Temitayo Osinubi or Temi for short and today I have the distinct honor and privilege to interview first-team SEO All-Star Mr. Michael King of ipullrank.com. Mike King is a Digital Marketing consultant specializing in SEO, content strategy, social media and measurement. Now that last part, measurement is what we're going to focus on because today's interview is about web analytics and reporting. So Mike, thanks so much for taking the time.

MK: Thanks for having me Temi. Always happy to help. Really excited to be here.

TO: Thank you, I greatly appreciate it. So how did you find your way to being a Digital Marketing consultant?

MK: So, it was completely by accident. When I was younger I was really into computers and things and I went to school for computer science. But midway, not midway, towards the end of that after doing some internships I realized that I would prefer to be a rap star instead. And so that's what I did.

I was an independent rap artist for about eight years, then in 2006 I got into a bicycle accident. Not even something cool like a motorcycle accident, but a bicycle accident. And I had to get a job to pay my medical bills. And the first place to hire me was an SEO agency because of my coding abilities.

So it's been about eight years now since then and I kinda got bit by the bug; I'd guess you'd say. I just really enjoy all things digital, all things marketing. And so moving on from the SEO agency I've worked in-house, I worked at a couple multinational ad agencies. I've worked at a couple boutique search firms and then recently I started my own shop. So, that's where I'm at.

TO: Cool, cool! That's a very exciting journey. What is your current role at your company and what do you do on a day-to-day basis?

MK: Sure, so my role is, I'm the founder so I'm responsible for everything. But also I'm a direct consultant, so I'm not somebody who just owns a company. I'm someone who does things. So there is no standard day-to-day. Some days I can be caught up in sales calls all day. Other days I could be writing code for a client. Other days I can be helping with creating content and coming up with strategies. Or it could just be a day where I'm sitting around doing reports, so it's some of everything, and for me it's a lot of fun because I don't get bored.

TO: Cool, cool! Nothing wrong with that. So name two web analytics resources and not software packages, so I'm talking about blogs, websites, articles, books etc. I'm not like Google Analytics or Omniture;

nothing like that. Two that you would recommend, one that you would not recommend.

MK: Well the second half of that is gonna be kinda difficult, but I would say that, you know, all signs points to Avinash Kaushik. He is the guy you want to be reading on a regular basis if you want to be in the know as far as analytics. So he has a great book, I can't remember the name of it right now. But I think it's called *Web Analytics* or something like that?

TO: *Web Analytics 2.0*, that's actually our textbook for this month.

MK: That's his second book; he had a book before that. But both books are great. I would say check out his stuff; also check out his blog. Since I already understand the basics of analytics, for me it's more valuable to read people who are more focused on things like conversion rate optimization.

So I really love the UnBounce blog. There's a guy named Peep Laja. I'm probably saying his name wrong. It's P-E-E-P L-A-J-A. He has a great blog too. Just, for me it's really about looking at conversion stuff, so those two blogs are a great place to start and the things they link to are generally really good as well. The Moz blog is good. There's a lot of that going on there. Um, Distilled.net, they talk about it a lot on their blog, so I would say start with those.

As far as what not to do? Well no, one more you should check out, so um, I know they recently changed the name of this but Google's

Conversion University is also really awesome. They're calling it something else now, but if you look up Conversion University you'll find it.

But uh, what would I not do? Yeah, I don't know! Ha, ha. I don't know what I would say as far as like what to avoid. I would say that reading things is important but the most important thing is that you play around with stuff. So it's one thing to read about analytics, but it's another thing to start your own blog, and ya know, throw GA on the site and see what happens. Ya know, play with it; really get to know it.

TO: Okay cool! Very sound advice, very good recommendations. Do you prefer free analytics tools like Google Analytics or do you like paid options like Cick Tale and why?

MK: So, I love Google Analytics because I love the ease of use. I love that it's standardized. I love that so many people use it. I love that it integrates with so many things, like, there's so many tools that, you know, you just click "hey, let me import my Google Analytics and now it's here." Setup is pretty easy as well. Google has plenty of tools; they have the Google tag manager now. Like GA is definitely my favorite way to go. I definitely prefer it over like, Adobe Analytics or Omniture or something that.

But there are also a variety of other tools that help with like, cohort analysis that are great! So Lucky Orange is my favorite one right now, and what it'll do is it'll videotape the session of the user. So you can go back and see what people are doing when they come to the site through different channels and specifically watch it. And then you can get a sense of what usability issues you're having and things like that. So there's a variety of tools that do things like that, ya know; KISSmetrics does a lot of cool stuff with heat mapping and things like that. So there are definitely use cases for all those different types of tools, but my favorite right now is Lucky Orange.

TO: Cool, cool. Lucky Orange; see that's excellent. I've never heard that before. I gotta go check it out. What skill set would you say is most important for an aspiring web analyst?

MK: I'd say curiosity! You know, like, of course having quantitative analysis skills is really important; of course using Excel, being able to bring data into focus when you're looking at a variety of data sets in comparison to your analytic, these are very valuable skills; but ultimately it's the curiosity that sets apart a good analyst from a great analyst. And really you have to understand what these numbers mean.

There are a lot of people that are happy with doing their standard reports and what have you; but if you don't have the curiosity to keep digging until you find an **insight** then you're probably not going to be a great analyst. So, I guess what I'm saying is that everything is important from the standard hard skills as far as, you know, being able to do statistics is really helpful as well.

What I'm really into now, or getting more into now is predicted analytics and that's a skill set that requires programming, it requires quantitative analysis, it requires an understanding of the platforms that you're using, but if you don't have that curiosity you're not going to find something that isn't standard out-of-the-box.

TO: Sage advice, very sage advice. So if you were to continue in your current role how would you like your position to evolve over time?

MK: Well I'm the boss, so I love it! It evolves in whatever way I want it to go. And that's the best part of it for me because I feel like in roles I've had in the past where it's been primarily SEO or whatever it is, everything is so siloed and my skill set is so broad that when you stick me in and say "Okay just do my meta tags for SEO" it's difficult for me; I just get bored.

So what I would like to see in my role is, right now I'm doing a ton of work. I would of course like to see my team grow so then I don't have to do so much "boots on the ground work." There are certain things that I'm doing right now that I don't love to do, but that have to be done because I want to make sure the work is great.

So I wanna be more like a player-coach, rather than the player and the coach; like someone who is a player and a coach at the same time. Like, I'm on the floor making plays but also handing the ball off to people that I know can make plays as well. So, I wanna see growth with the business. I wanna be able to step back and work with people I can

161

trust.

TO: Absolutely! Nothing wrong with that. So that leads into my next question; Where do you see the Digital Marketing industry as a whole, but web analytics in particular, going over the next five to ten years?

MK: Yeah, I think everything is gonna get increasingly more personalized and increasingly more automated; and people are gonna get a lot more effective at doing those things. Cuz one of the problems with automation right now is that people don't know how to do it right and make it still have the personal touch. There's a lot of things that are being automated and people can tell that they're obviously automated, and they're not really speaking to that person. And with the amount of data that we have these days it's just getting more easy to do it the right way.

And you know, the better we get with employing more data scientists and building even better tools, things are just gonna get way more incredible; and the thing is that people are expecting this type of experience at this point because they know that there's so much data that they've given. They know that with FaceBook for instance, they're giving tons of data on things that they're interested in, and who they are, and what makes them tick. So people are expecting more experiences that are tailored to them.

The analytics role plays a HUGE part in this, because they are the people that bring back the insights and identify the specific cohorts within the data that are expecting something, or a given thing resonates with them more than another cohort; so analytics people are gonna to have to, again, be more curious and dig into that data and then surface those types of insights that's going to fuel the predictive modeling and personalization of the future.

TO: Very sage advice, as well I could not agree more. That's one of the reasons I'm so stoked about mobile, me personally, because what's more personal than your mobile device? Like most people I don't share that with anybody. I may share my computer, but that iPhone is all me!

So Michael, I greatly appreciate you taking the time to do this interview with me. Where can people get a hold of you if they need your services or just some advice?

MK: Yeah, sure. You can reach out at ipullrank.com. If you just want advice I'm on Clarity FM, also you can just reach out to me on Twitter. I'm pretty responsive, you know, I'm a busy guy but I always try to make time for people that need some help.

TO: Cool, cool! Well, this has been an interview with Digital Marketing consultant Michael King of ipullrank.com. Thanks so much!

MK: No problem.

Takeaways

- Make the numbers more fun by following the numbers like a treasure map.

- Remarketing is awesome.

- Mike King is awesomer!

For additional resources and content updates, please visit
ThinkBeyondBuzzwords.com/analytics

11

It's Getting Harder

"It's not even SEO anymore; it's traffic generation."

-Brett Burky
RadicallyAmbitious.com

Have we got a treat for you! Up to this point the *Killer Bees - Killer Content* interviews have been accompaniments to the chapter content. Not this time. This entire chapter, from beginning to end, is the unmitigated awesomeness that is a *Killer Bees - Killer Content* interview!

The original interview is 30 minutes long, which translates to 20 written pages. Rather than giving you a word-for-word transcription of this lengthy video, instead we've distilled the most salient parts. But if you insist on the blow-by-blow, you can check out the source video at the link below. Enjoy!

Interview Video Source: https://goo.gl/s9kUlr

From Blackhat to Master of Business Intelligence

I was first introduced to Brett Burky as the Professor for my PPC class at Full Sail University, and we hit it off instantly. His courses were always the funnest, yet very impactful. Digital Marketing may as well be on dog years for as fast as it progresses. To be a ten-year vet in this industry, you may as well have been doing it for the last 30 years. But to be a ten-year vet as well as teach SEO and PPC at a collegiate level; Brett has a unique vantage point few can lay claim to.

A musician by birth and a curious mind by condition, Brett has been challenging the way things are since he was getting suspended in high school. Starting the computer technology club in high school, Brett got the bug of tech and realized what was possible. His life led to playing music professionally for Disney. He moved to Tokyo and played professional music for Tokyo Disney.

He later played acts for Sony, but started to get tired of the late nights and heavy lifestyle that being a musician creates. He started his search online in 2003 for answers and started affiliate marketing.

Once back in the U.S. he paid his way to knowledge and has been at it ever since. Focusing on SEO and ranking the #1 spot for SEO consulting, he created a consulting business. But after dealing with a lot of "making others rich," he just recently started doing things for himself.

Currently he runs a completely automated business and now is able to focus on his dreams of what he always wanted to do, create greatness and be involved in long-term plays to take him to ultimate freedom. Brett is still creating systems and working with top underground guys that aren't in it for the recognition, instead they're in it for the ultimate thing – time freedom.

I picked Brett's beautiful mind about his past, present and where he sees the future of Digital Marketing going as it related to business intelligence. He was awesome enough to grace us with this chapter's *Killer Bees – Killer Content*.

Temitayo Osinubi = TO   **Brett Burky = BB**

TO: What was the atmosphere like back then, in terms of Internet Marketing?

BB: They didn't really call it SEO, I guess? It was weird. At that time, 2005/2006, everyone was all about real estate. I was like, "Yeah, I'm not doing that, because that's where everyone is at." And then after the real estate bust everyone started kind of talking about Internet marketing and SEO. I'd go to a place and I'd introduce myself, "I do Internet marketing and SEO," and they were like, "Oh, you're one of those guys?" And I was like, "No, no, no... I'm not a guy who was in real estate and then now I'm done with it and now I'm starting SEO. I've been doing this for a long time."

So, it was one of those things where they thought it was the new buzzword, and I was like, "No, this has already been around." But back then, you could test things and break things and you'd get real results. I remember I could just do interesting stuff. For local marketing, I would scrape Craigslist for all kinds of leads. That was one great thing I would do.

This is kind of blackhat, but they have these satellite offices in all of the United States for... I forget what it was called... but, I got one address in Orlando and I realized Google's algorithm was based around "where's the courthouse?" because that's going to be the most centralized location inside the city with the most centralized zip code. So I was like, "Alright, I'll get a satellite office in each one of these major cities with that zip code, and I'll rank my stuff like number one."

So we did that for Chicago, New York, LA... I can't remember... Dallas... I mean, we had 25 some cities we were doing all over the place. This is when you could log in and Google local was... actually, Omar's email was Mr. Local SEO. He kind of was doing it before it was happening and we had it all over. We'd do things like that and there was all kinds of ways of ranking things a lot easier.

That's when the article marketing was big. I would do little weird scripts, like write something in Google to find out what was the hottest ranking article in the last four months, because it had been seen this many times, how many views, and then we would use that.

It was a lot more free and open, and social media was not really existent. We didn't really care for social media. It was forums and then, you know with everything... it's different. SEO is not even SEO. People will say SEO and I'm like, "Yeah, it's not... just say traffic," you know? Because SEO is not... what I see they don't see, you know? It's not the same thing.

TO: Right, which leads me to my next question. How have things changed since then to now?

BB: Oh, it's changed a lot! Some of the stuff I would say you have to think differently in terms of what SEO means. If someone were to ask, "Hey, what do you do?", "Well, I do SEO." Well okay then... you're missing a part! You can't just say, "I do SEO." You do traffic generation. That's why if you look at my name, it says, "Traffic Strategist," because it's about how to get traffic; either as a paid method, is it drawing traffic from social, are you going to forums? It's not so much of "I rank things in Google" anymore, because nobody cares about that.

I mean, I don't care as much anymore because everything is generalized through either location, or past history of what you have searched previously with cookies etc. They have it now to where search results can change based on the cookies on the website you have actually visited. There are all kinds of things where that doesn't work anyone. So, I think it's changed to where now you have to focus on what is the traffic strategy and how do I get the most traffic; and not worry about rankings as much.

You know the funny thing is, people still want to see it. Clients will say, "Oh, where are we ranked." I say, "Well, you're ranked good," because no one has ever actually logged in and searched for you before.

TO: Excellent. So, I said at the beginning of the interview, you just got a Master's Degree in Business Intelligence. For those of you who don't know, business intelligence is basically if you've ever gone to Amazon and it says at the bottom, "people who bought this also bought that," or if you just started following somebody on Twitter, you might get an email from Twitter saying. "Based on you following person X, we think you might like person Y."

So, how has "Big Data" changed how you operate as an Internet Marketer?

BB: It gets you better analytics, for one. You're able to get a lot more information. Understanding how to extract it and know what to do with it is the crux that you have to figure out. How you use it is where it takes some skill to really think, "Okay, now I got all this information, what does this mean?" You know? Just because I have it doesn't mean I can do anything with it.

So, there are the different parts of it. Understanding how to extract things, how to make the crawler and find... well here's an example. YouTube, just last April I think... they allowed you to advertise on individual videos. My daughter will watch *Ninja Turtles*. She loves *Ninja Turtles*. So, she is watching *Ninja Turtles* and there's an ad for like State Farm. I'm like, they're not doing this right. My daughter does not care about State Farm. If someone wanted to advertise correctly, they'd advertise *Ninja Turtle* toys or something like that, if they were hitting it right. But that's because people do blanket ads they just say, "Advertise on everything on YouTube. That's dumb. Unless you have lots of money, like State Farm.

For somebody like me, they allowed you to advertise strictly on one video, one URL, which is called site placement on regular Adwords, but it just started last year in YouTube. I was like, this is great! So being able to type in something, setting my search limits over 100, and then creating a crawler using something called Data Import IO, crawl all of these and I want to advertise on all these videos.

That's basically kind of "Big Data" because you're taking thousands of URLs and being able to upload. That's one aspect of it. That's data extraction, which is maybe the beginning part of how to use more data in your Internet marketing. Then being able to load it into something, I guess would be the ETL system of loading it in, but I'm only loading it into Adwords. That's where I've used a lot of things from what I learned in the Business Intelligence degree to be able to use in my day-to-day Internet marketing stuff.

TO: So as you continue to see data proliferate at an increasing rate, in your professional opinion, do you think it's reasonable to think that you can just fire off and start Internet marketing without any professional training, or do you think with the current state of things you should invest in some education?

BB: I think you have to invest in education; just from my own education before I came to Full Sail. There are still parts where I'll see something, but when it's structured and you go to a structured system, you get it the right way. With me, it was kind of like I need to figure out how to do this, so I'd figure out how to do that, but then it's hodgepodge. There's missing gaps in my knowledge because it wasn't a structured. I would learn techniques, but I didn't see the overall picture.

Although I teach, I know what I know really well, but I don't know some of the other professor's classes, like branding. I won't speak eloquently about anything branding-wise. But I think if you have the overall education, you can look at things a little bit more objectively.

For me, I'm one of those guys that focus more on "let's get it up, let's get it going, and let's get some traffic, test it and see if it's working." If it's working, then we will go back and make it pretty and do all the stuff for branding it. That pre-branding stuff drives me nuts! Let's get the business cards; let's make sure we have a perfect logo, let's spend $500. We don't even know if this works yet! Let's just get it going, let's just write our name in pencil, just put it up there. Let's market first, test the idea, then go back and if it's working okay, let's invest some stuff in the other things.

So because of that, I miss a lot of the parts because I never spent any time with it. So having a structured idea you'd probably be better, at least I think so. And in this day and age, too, having education from people that actually know what they're doing and not trying to push an agenda.

I mean, you get a lot of these Internet marketers guys . . . I feel sorry for a lot of people. Warrior Forum; it's like ugh! I know some of these people and I have seen the inside game and how it works. I'm like, you guys are just not right! Just some of things they do and how they promote each other... the whole Guru mentality; people get sucked into that.

There's no Guru mentality with actual education, from people who have done it.

TO: Right. So as a whole, how would you describe the industry of Internet marketing?

BB: I think there are different levels. I think there are different areas of Internet marketing. There is Internet marketing for business people, and the thing is, with Internet marketing, sometimes there are proprietary things they are not going to let go. If I know something that is working, why would I tell the world?

A lot of times when those things are let go, it's because they are starting to not work anymore. That's why these people make these products, or you know, they launch something after it's already been done. It's been done for the last year or two, now it's not working, now let's go ahead and sell it.

Perfect example, and I think he is a brilliant marketer; Ryan Deiss, they have Survival Life. So he's selling how his system works, but it's because that whole prepare mentality thing is kind of over. After 2012 I guess people were like, "Well I guess the world's not going to end. So what do I have like 90 barrels of rice over here for?" So they could see the traffic go down, so they are like, "Okay, well this is kind of going downhill, let's go ahead and make a product on how to do what we did."

So you're getting a lot of the stuff after the fact. What's actually happening currently, and what a lot of people are getting in terms of education is past the mark. Sometimes; and sometimes you'll get what's happening now. I think a lot of times with the Internet marketing industry, you just have to be in there. Some of the best people I know, they don't listen to a lot of people. The data tells them what's working.

No one is going to tell you they know Google's algorithm. They just don't! And you can't believe everything that Matt Cutts says. I just say focus on what you're doing, how does it work for your industry, and that's what I think would be the best.

Some of these guys that have Internet marketing products and stuff like that, they have a high, high overhead. I mean, Frank Kern, just for his child support alone has to make a $50,000 nut every month (a monthly nut is just your monthly expenses). So, do you think sometimes his marketing might get a little bit swayed just so he can cover his bases? That's the way I see it, test it on your own.

TO: And I tell people all the time, because there is this school of thought, not everybody is on board with the concept of getting a degree in Internet marketing. They think the industry changes to often, it's too broad etc. But like I tell folks, it really is the wild, wild web! It's kind of a no-man's land. You might stumble across Avinash Kaushik, or you might stumble across a blackhat? In some areas it's a proper cesspool, so this idea that you can just follow the right people on Twitter... I mean yeah you can, but you have to know who to follow.

BB: Yeah, you're right.

TO: So, it's not quite as simple as that, and thanks for that. That's some really sage advice. So, you've been doing this since 2005, coming up on ten years, so you know, you're a seasoned vet. Do you prefer the "good old days" of Internet marketing or do you think that the best days are ahead, and why?

BB: I think they're just different. I mean it's more genuine now than it was before. Before you could game it a lot more, now you can't game it. They are using semantic indicators and it's not so much that I can sit behind the computer and just type out stuff and rank things anymore.

They're using all these different metrics in terms of how your brand is perceived through different words. They're text mining all the ways that people are saying anything around certain websites to understand, should these people actually rank. They're using analytics in their favor. If your sites ranks number one, but you have a 70% bounce rate, and the time on site is garbage; they're going to look at these things. That process is automated to where they are going to say there's no authenticity to this site, why is this ranking number one?

I think the days where you can get away with a lot of stuff is over. The days of not building a brand and actually being authentic is done, and it needs to be done! Because it's just not right, and not only that, it's stressful! I did stuff back in the day where we had 150 websites and you have all your money riding on it. Every night you're wondering, "Well, I wonder if today will be the day that Google slaps you down?" and now everything you have is gone.

Plus thinking in terms of only what Google cares about is dumb! I mean, Google is a great thing; but if Google were gone tomorrow you really want to make sure that's not your only ball of wax. Like okay, "Do I have an audience, do I have an email list, do I have a proper social following, am I an authority on this, do I have any other content out there on podcasts, do I have stuff out there on SlideShare?" Do people know me from different angles, and if I rank in Google that's great but, but that's not my only thing.

So I think before, it was all about Google and now it's about traffic. It's a totally different ball of wax. Google is one piece of it, Bing is a smaller piece of it, but by the same idea, I find more stuff from interesting people that are referred to me. I pay attention to people I think are authorities and when they say something, I'll look at it.

Like one girl, Ann Smarty, she's a great, great SEO, runs Internet Marketing Ninjas. She is out of St. Pete, Florida here. She always has great stuff, and I always pay attention to it. For SEO information, I go to Inbound.org. So it's not so much I go to search Google anymore.

If I want to find something about SEO, I go to Inbound.org and it's always the best stuff. I know there's certain websites to find the certain information; you know what I mean? So it's a totally different ball of wax, and it's better. It's a harder process now, but it will stand longer the test of time, and you'll have a business. That's the way I see it.

Which is kind of interesting, because it's all personal branding, so I guess that can go two different ways, too. If you personally brand yourself, you can't sell yourself, and if you destroy your personal brand, you're only one person. So before, you could actually have 150 websites and no one knows who you were. There is no name to it, there's no authority, there's nothing to it. It's just website ranks.

Now, it's you are the website, you go along with whatever it is and there is a lot more involved in terms of your reputation, so that's the only... I wouldn't say bad thing, but the thing to be aware of. What you say reflects on your brand.

TO: Excellent. That's some really deep insight. So, almost done and I appreciate your time. So, you dropped some really good nuggets, the Inbound.org and all that good stuff. So, if there's someone who wants to start, but for whatever reason they're in a life situation to where they can't drop $50,000 on a Bachelor's, where would you suggest that they start?

BB: If I was to start over and basically say lock yourself in a room for three weeks and read this, and then take notes on it, then go do it . . . I would say go to DistilledU. Actually SEO Moz, this is their SEO team; Distilled.

So they have a thing called DistilledU, which is like a gamification thing where you can go through and learn all about SEO and different parts of marketing. I would go there.

I would go to Learn With Google go through all the webinars, go through their training, take the tests, get that idea, understand how it works.

And then lastly, I would go to Neil Patel. Neil Patel has... I think he calls them definitive guides. If you just type in "definitive guide + Neil Patel" he has everything on content marketing, paid search, social marketing etc. And these things are huge, I mean they're like 10 pages long and they're lengthy. If you went through all that and then you went through all those trainings, understood it. Then getting in with a good forum so you can have some people that can mentor you, finding the right people. That's really important and it really matters where you're trying to go.

One of my favorite forums a lot of people don't know about, and I don't think they want it that way, but it's called Dynamite Circle. These guys, a lot of them are expats that live all over south Asia. They run E-Commerce stores and they send stuff here.

I learned some of the best things from those guys, but it's because they're testing things, they're doing things, and they're real dudes. Webmaster World, that's an old, old, old forum. I don't even know if they allow people in anymore.

If you're in that, that's a good forum, and then that's pretty much what I would do. Because then you get the basis of who are the people that are actually doing the real deal right now that I can learn from them. And then having a project, because it means nothing to learn it if you don't do it. That's the way I feel. It's like, you can read all you want about learning how to play guitar, but until you pick it up, it doesn't matter.

TO: Right, right. This has been absolutely amazing, Brett. Thank you so much. If someone wanted to hire you for traffic generation or just pick that awesome brain of yours, where can they find you?

BB: I'm at radicallyambitious.com.

TO: Radicallyambitious.com. Well there you have it folks. This has been an interview with radically ambitious, Master of Business Intelligence, Mr. Brett Burky. Thanks so much, Brett. I appreciate it.

BB: Yeah, man. This was fun.

Takeaways

- SEO isn't SEO anymore, it's traffic generation.

- Worry about what the traffic strategy is and not rankings as much.

- Big data gives you better analytics.
- Digital Marketing is more genuine now than it was before.

For additional resources and content updates, please visit
ThinkBeyondBuzzwords.com/evolving-marketplace

12

The Hardest Pill to Swallow

"The choice is between multiplication of results using strengths or incremental improvement fixing weaknesses that will, at best, become mediocre. Focus on better use of your best weapons instead of constant repair."

- Timothy Ferriss,

The 4-Hour Workweek

Sometimes you need to know when to call it quits. This is especially true if you are running a business. If you are new to this, allow me to save you a whole lot of heartache and pain. You CANNOT do it all. You simply cannot. There will never be enough hours in a day for you to do all things and to do them at a professional level. This is where time leveraging comes into play.

Time leveraging is exactly what it sounds like. You buy time from willing, and of age, participants. These participants typically do things you are either unable or unwilling to do. Ok, that did sound a little creepy, but let me explain.

Even if you are not a business owner you do this all of the time and you probably don't think twice about it. Prime example, you come home and your living room is a swimming pool. I'm not talking about a blow up kiddie pool out of a big box store. No. Your entire living room is in fact a swimming pool, and not just any swimming pool. Noooo, a surprise swimming pool! At this point you have a few options:

A. Walk out the door like nothing happened. You may have to skip town and change your name.

B. Call a plumber.

C. Stand in the surprise swimming pool and cry.

D. Call your cousins Ray-Ray and Man-Man and y'all try to fix it yourselves.

Options A and C don't fix the problem, they only make the problem worse. Option D, depending on the skill level of Ray-Ray and Man-Man and the availability of tools, may cause a bigger, and more expensive problem later on. Option B, for most people, would be the best solution.

The surprise swimming pool, may seem to be an extreme example to some, but that's what I see when I look at some businesses and their marketing.

They will pretend like they don't have a marketing problem, because they have "word of mouth," and they are barely making enough money to keep the lights on. They cry about how great their business would be if they could just get their marketing together, but then refuse to take marketing actions. Or, my favorite one, they have the "I got a guy" mentality.

"I got a guy," in Digital Marketing typically refers to a small business owner's father, niece, nephew, or a friend from down the block who at took that one class on marketing four years ago in college before he dropped out to pursue an acting career. If you're laughing right now you probably have, or know someone that has the "I got a guy" mentality. For clarity's sake, I'm not harping on your poor second cousin twice removed. They may actually have some marketing skills. However, in my experience when 20-year-old Ray-Ray, Man-Man, or Booky is put in charge of marketing it typically doesn't go too well. The end result is usually inconsistent, the marketing is usually overpriced, the targeting is

184

off, and you can't find "that guy" when you need him. I could go on and on, but I think you got the point. Bottom-line, the results are lackluster and you don't know any better to do any better.

It's like when I was in undergrad and had the opportunity to travel to a behavior analysis conference that was hosted in a five-star hotel. Up to that point I had only known one and two-star motels. Don't get me wrong, there's nothing wrong with a motel with it's scratchy, probably infested sheets, its leaky faucets, and midnight shootouts; my aunt has worked in a very popular motel for decades. However, *I* will never willingly stay in a motel again after experiencing the luxury and comfort of a five-star hotel.

Reeling it back in; above, option B was the best choice because you kept your, and more importantly, your property's best interest at heart. By calling on and paying an expert with the right tools, knowledge and experience to get the job done, you've also just obligated them to work in a timely and professional manner. That directly correlates to how you handle your marketing.

Moral of the story, if you are in a dark alley and a stranger asks to check your prostate, don't do it! Go seek a professional and avoid a lot of heartache and pain.

I'm no gypsy mind reader, but I'm guessing that you are thinking what I was thinking not too long ago. That is: "I can't afford to hire someone to do my marketing, and I surely can't hire one of those big named companies either." Well you're in luck, because you don't have to do either of those things.

First things first, I want to quickly touch on the ideas of "Afford" and "Expensive." I'm going to get to all of the juicy stuff, but just flow with me for a few minutes.

The words "Afford" and "Expensive" in everyday language typically have nothing to do with cost. It's all about the perceived value of a product or service.

If your customer perceives the market value of your product at $100 and you have it priced at $600, they aren't going to buy because it's too "expensive." Whereas if your product is priced at $600 and the customer places a mental value of $1,000 on that product, they can't have you take their money fast enough.

Quick example: I have a carrot stand. I'm selling each carrot for $30, I am the only carrot stand around for 500 miles. Would you buy a carrot? Probably not, you'd say it was too expensive.

New scenario: I have a carrot stand. I'm selling each carrot for $50, I am the only carrot stand around for 500 miles, and all the rest of the food on the planet is poison. How many carrots would you like to buy?

The item didn't change, but the perceived value of the item did. Once your target market is able to see the true value in your product or service, you will never have to hear "I can't afford that," or "That's too expensive." You may start to hear, "Why is it so cheap?" As soon as you get this concept it will take your business to all new heights.

This doesn't have to be relegated just to business; I use this concept in my day-to-day life as well. Spending over $300 a month for a personal trainer seemed expensive, at first. Then when I realized that the medical bills, junk food, and lack of overall happiness I got from NOT losing weight, I quickly swiped my credit card. Sometimes when the first thought is, "I can't afford that!" the very next thought should be, "Can I afford not to have that?" the answer and results may surprise you.

Now that's out of the way, here comes the juice.

The solution to your marketing dilemma is...wait for it...Outsourcing! Outsourcing, is the best way to get things done without hiring a new employee and better yet, not doing it yourself. You may have heard of outsourcing before, sometimes they are called virtual assistants. What I'm going to do in the next few paragraphs is really map out the process for you. I'm going to tell you where to go, who to hire, how much to pay, and how to protect your ass...ets. So, grab your highlighter and let's go!

Where to Go

There are many great places online to find top talent to outsource to. The ones that I am most familiar with are:

- Upwork.com (formally Odesk)

- Elance.com
- Fiverr.com

For the quick and easy jobs like, making a graphic, doing a logo, writing an article, or quick keyword research, fiverr.com is the best place to go. If you need something like a 15-page exposé on a topic in your industry for your email marketing campaign, you should use Elance.com. To get a website built, a marketing campaign designed/implemented, or anything else that requires "heavy lifting," Upwork.com would be your best bet.

Like I said earlier, there are many places that have outsourcing directories; these three are the ones I suggest because I've hired people on them (bought time) and sold my own services on them (sold time). If you find another place that works for you, by all means stick with it.

Who to Hire

On all of these websites, the contractors have profiles that give user rating, typically expressed in stars, past jobs done, and testimonials from previous people who've hired that contractor. In the case of Fiverr.com, most jobs are $5 with additional add ons, but in the case of Upwork.com you can view the contractors average requested rate as well as the average rate they have worked for in the past. So, how do you pick one? As with everything in Digital Marketing, it depends.

What services do you need? If you find yourself needing 20 different things, prioritize that list and pick the first one. Next, does this person have contact with your customers? If the answer is no, then anyone with the skill set from any country will do. If the answer is yes, and you live in America, I'd try to find someone that is from America and/or speaks English clearly. If you are hiring this person for customer support and they don't have verbal communication skills, just make sure that they are able to type clearly. On Upwork, freelancers are required to take certain tests. English, grammar, and spelling are a few of the tests they have to take. So when in doubt, check to see if they've taken the tests. If they have, check their scores. If it's a B+ or higher they are pretty good.

Bonus: Don't Forget About Good Ole' Networking

Networking, true networking seems to be a lost art. I know early in the chapter I talked about not having your father, nieces, nephews, cousins, or friend from down the block do your marketing. However, networking with the intent to find a professional Digital Marketer is very different.

The higher level networking activities I'm speaking about are meet-ups, small business gatherings like the ones your local chamber puts together, and even industry specific conferences. Check out meetup.com to find an assortment of small and large gatherings in your local area.

How Much to Charge

If you are working with a limited budget and you have a firm number in mind for your project, I say put that number out there and see who bites. If no one bites adjust the number a bit and wait. If you have no idea what to charge, type the service you want in the search bar and see what other people have paid individuals for a similar project. If the number is in your ballpark, put it out there and see who bites. While searching if you find someone who has already done that project in the past, they are in your price range and they have received 4.5 stars or higher, just hire them. Send them a direct message with the job details and give them two business days to reply. If they accept, congratulations you've hired your first contractor!

One important piece of information to remember is: "Don't forget to negotiate." If your budget is $20/hr and the perfect person wants $25/hr start at $16 and land somewhere around $22. It's a little over budget, but for the right person it's worth it.

Protecting Your Assets

It doesn't matter if you are a business owner with a storefront or if you are a solopreneur that works from your kitchen table, keep in mind that at the end of the day, your business is well... a business. The following section will teach you how to protect yourself when doing business.

Tip 1: Nondisclosures

Always have your freelancers/contractors sign a Nondisclosure Agreement. You never want to have to worry about people telling or selling your business secrets.

Tip 2: Contracts, Contracts, Contracts!

Always have your contractor sign a contract. Most freelancing platforms already have some type of service rendering contract that both you and the contractor agree to before they take the job. However, I alway advise to go the extra step. You can never have too much legal protection when it comes to your business.

The contract should outline **exactly** what the project entails, the day their contract is over, **exactly** how much they are to be paid, and when they are to be paid. In addition you may want to outline that they are **NOT** an employee and therefore are not entitled to any employee benefits. If you are unsure of any of these details don't ignore them. Address them in such a way that covers your business.

For example, if you are hiring someone for a simple project, but you aren't sure how long the project will take write something like:

"The contract will be terminated when all items on the fulfillment list are satisfied to the standards of management."

A common question is: "Can I combine Tips 1 and 2?" My common answer is "No." Sentences like the one above and any other language that speaks of termination should never be on the same page as a nondisclosure unless you are a lawyer or you are 100% sure that the words you've chosen will hold up in court.

Tip 3: Give them the Key, but Control the Lock

One of the worst things in the world, besides realizing that you've left your wallet on the kitchen table once you've made it halfway to the store, is paying someone for a project, (i.e. digital art, article writing, producing a video etc.) getting the items you've paid for and not having access to the originals. What usually happens months down the line is that you'll find something that you want to edit. This could mean expanding an image, adding text to a banner ad, changing words on a video, or any number of things. This isn't a problem. Expanding, reusing, and editing already-made content is a practice of good business. The problem is the person you've hired is long gone and the odds of you getting access to the originals are slim to none. Depending on the severity of the change, you may have to start from scratch and get the items created again. This wastes precious time and money. The best way to nip this problem in the bud is to get the originals before the contract is over. Most people won't have a problem with providing drafts and originals, but just to cover your assets, put it in the contract.

Besides protecting the intellectual property you've paid for, you want to make sure that you can give and restrict access to any platforms or websites. For example, if you hire someone to handle your social media make sure you give them a dedicated password. Once the contract is over simply turn off or deactivate the password to the account. The last thing you want to have is someone no longer associated with your company with backend access to your website or social media accounts.

Tip 4: Back Those Things Up

Back in undergrad I could have sworn that my red Toshiba laptop was demon possessed! Every time without fail, if I was in a rush, cramming for a test moments before class, or trying to get an online assignment turned in on a Sunday at 11:59:59 P.M. my computer would crash. Those 20-page, expertly typed papers would evaporate into the cyber ether.

This is not something you want to happen in your business. So, please, please, please, make sure you backup your content to an off site server. There are plenty of cloud storage options out there; a simple Google search will bring up some of the top guys. I personally back everything up on my personal server. If you are looking for a free option, every Gmail account comes with 15GB of cloud space. It's called Google Drive. You can store, share, and create documents all in the drive for free. So now you have no reason not to do it.

Getting Too Big for Your Freelancer?

If you've been in business for a while and your company is a bit bigger than you and your first five guys, you may have needs greater than what an average freelancer can provide. There's nothing wrong with that, and as always I have a solution.

You may want to consider a small to mid size Digital Marketing firm.

You are going to want to keep some of the same considerations in mind when hiring a consulting firm as you would a contractor from Upwork.com. Make sure they are experienced and trustworthy. Check their educational backgrounds. If the leadership has degrees in American History or Aztec Pottery, that may not be the best company to meet your needs.

Another thing to check for is certifications. You want to make sure the company and its leadership are Google Adwords, Bing Ads, and Google Analytics Certified if they are doing your SEO, and /or PPC marketing. If they are building a website, make sure you ask to see their latest portfolio.

If they don't have customer reviews on their website or social media pages, make sure to ask about previous clients.

You are going to have to interview these firms like they are going to be your next employee. While "interviewing," make sure to ask about customer service. Know who to speak to if you have any questions. Know if you are going to have a dedicated person on your account or if you are always going to have to go through a "portal" to speak with someone about your business's projects.

When it comes to price, make sure expectations are clear. Go back to the "Affordable" and "Expensive" theory I wrote about in the beginning of this chapter. Make sure the ROI is there before committing to a marketing firm.

Lastly if you are on the fence about taking on a firm, ask for a trial or a test project. Most rational companies will give you a 30-120 day trial/contract or they'll do a test job, so that you, as a business owner will feel more comfortable about signing longer 1 and 2-year contracts.

Just to recap: If you are not an expert in whatever you are doing, and you have a little bit of money to get the job done, hire someone to do it. Make sure that the person you hire has the necessary tools and skill set to get the job done. Protect your assets by having contracts signed and in hand before hiring or paying anyone. Make sure that you control the backend access to your platforms and you are able to get your hands on the originals if need be. Lastly don't forget to backup your data.

If your company has gotten too big for the average freelancer, seek out a reputable marketing firm that can handle your needs.

Takeaways

- Save time and money by getting the job outsourced.

- Afford and Expensive are based off of perceived value.

- Protect your ass...ets with contracts.

- If you are too big for the average freelancer, interview a marketing firm.

  Pssst. 1-855-WEB-WORK (932-9675) ... Just sayin'.

For additional resources and content updates, please visit
ThinkBeyondBuzzwords.com/outsourcing

Conclusion

Wow! That was a lot to digest, right? We know what you must be thinking, "Now what, Michelle and Temi? You guys wrote all those pages, shared all this insight; now what?" But before that, some fun facts:

- Global ad spend will reach $540 billion in 2015, up 4% from 2014 and it's expected to climb another 5% in 2016.
- Of that $540 billion, digital ad spend makes up almost 24% or $129 billion.
- That's still only ½ of TV ad spend.
- By some estimates, digital ad spend will overtake TV as soon as 2018.
- Digital ad spend is fueled mostly by mobile and video.

"Okay... so...?"

The point is this pie known as Digital Marketing is almost unfathomably HUGE and it's getting bigger by the day. By virtue of the fact you did us the high honor of reading to the very end, we know you could stand to have a bigger piece of that global $540 billion pie.

Heck, we could too! But that is never going to happen until the foolishness stops! Again, we love this industry and all of the transformational promise it holds. But we hate how it's become a haven for a lot of bad actors.

So if you're self-taught, or a small to medium size business owner that does your own Digital Marketing, we hope we've helped you think and perform at a higher level. If you have aspirations of pursuing Digital Marketing as a career we implore you to seek professional training. Again, we're biased towards degrees, but not boogie.

As part of your purchase of this book you have free access to our resource website where we keep up-to-date with industry trends and continue to hone our craft. It took a combined investment approaching $150,000 in tuition, degrees and other programs to build the context needed to curate these resources, and it's yours free for being part of our community.

Pretty benevolent, huh? Yes, yes it does take a certain caliber of conscientiousness and sense of duty to the industry to act in such a philanthropic, laudable, and awe-inspiring manner... putting the grandiose sarcasm aside; we truly believe a rising tide lifts all ships. HOWEVER, if your boat (skill set) has a gaping hole in it, or better yet you don't even have a real boat but a raft made out of driftwood, that rising tide isn't going to benefit you much if you're shipwrecked on the bottom of the sea!

So instead of setting you loose against an ever-expanding tsunami of content; a deluge of data, the likes of which the world has never seen before, then having the unmitigated gall to tell you to "take it with a grain of salt," if we've done our jobs you should now know what in fact salt tastes like with regard to Digital Marketing. You should be able to think beyond buzzwords. That context is priceless and increasingly more difficult to come by.

THANK YOU for allowing us to be your guides. Please visit the resource section for a list of recommended training and degree programs. We look forward to inspiring you to awesomeness.

Buzzwords & Terms

Whether you're a do-it-yourselfer or Digital Marketing pro, if you spend any significant time at all in the space you're going to hear these terms thrown around more than a little. Following are what we consider just a smatter of buzzwords to be aware of. These definitions are in our own words, as well as their definition from the venerable Wikipedia and other sources.

This list by no means is meant to be exhaustive or all encompassing. As new words come onto the scene we'll be sure to update the resources section.

Buzzwords

Actionable Analytics: Analytics that uncover insights and inform data-driven decisions, as opposed to analytics for the sake of analytics.

Advertainment: Advertising that doubles as entertainment, but in a natural, non-ironic way (e.g. *Transformers* is basically one big GM commercial, but it doesn't feel like it because you're too busy watching Optimus Prime and Bumble Bee kick butt!

Agile Marketing: Marketing initiatives that are quick and nimble (agile) and allow for real time adjustments.

Authenticity: Faking it is even less acceptable online. Be yourself... or else!

Big Data: A collection of data sets so large and complex it becomes difficult to manage and requires new and powerful tools.

Brand Storytelling: A content marketing methodology that states as technology evolves, so do users' expectations of how content will be delivered to them, but never at the expense of good storytelling.

Customer-centricity: Putting the customer at the center of your brand strategy, activity and analysis.

Connected Living: Ubiquitous connectivity, anytime, anywhere via a combination of devices and services that integrate video, voice, and data services.

Content is King: Overused catch phrase that emphasizes how essential it is to have a good content strategy.

Contextual Marketing: Advertising designed to align with the media property in which it appears.

Earned Media: Second party distribution of your message with no cost to you.

Engagement Marketing: A marketing strategy that directly engages consumers and invites and encourages consumers to participate in the evolution of the brand.

Gamification: The systems and processes that drive engagement by turning extrinsic rewards into intrinsic rewards.

Growth Hacking: A marketing technique developed by technology startups, which use creativity, analytical thinking, and social metrics to sell products and gain exposure.

Immersive Design: The activity of a new generation of designers who work inclusively across all story-driven media.

Internet of Things or IoT: Uniquely identifiable objects and their virtual representations in an Internet-like structure.

Localization: The movement towards optimizing for consumers with local buying intent.

Millennials: Also known as Generation Y; a cohort born between 1982 and 2004.

Mobile Optimization: Providing a good user experience on a small screen. Your mobile site/app should NOT require the users to pinch and zoom on their mobile device.

Native Advertising: This is sponsored content; an online advertising method in which the advertiser attempts to gain attention by providing content in the context of the user's experience.

Neuromorphics: Building and training computers to think like humans do.

Newsjacking: Injecting your brand ideas into breaking news stories, thereby hijacking the associated traffic and social media engagement.

Onmi-channel Retailing: The evolution of multi-channel retailing, but concentrated more on a seamless approach to the consumer experience through all available shopping channels.

Programmatic Marketing: Marketing campaigns that are automatically triggered by any type of event and deployed according to a set of rules applied by software algorithms.

Rich Media: Traditionally describes display (banner) advertising that expands to offer interactive elements.

Responsive Web Design: A web design approach aimed at crafting sites that deliver an optimal viewing experience, regardless of device or screen size.

Selfie: A type of self-portrait photograph, typically taken with a hand-held digital camera or camera phone.

SoLoMo: An inclusive term that describes three big marketing trends, social media, local commerce and mobile.

Snackable Content: Bite-sized chunks of information that can quickly be consumed by the audience.

Showrooming: The practice of viewing an item in a physical store, then later purchasing it online for a lower price.

Social Commerce: New online retail models or marketing strategies that incorporates established social networks and/or peer-to-peer communication to drive sales.

Second-Screen: Describes viewing content on one device (a tablet, smartphone or computer) that provides contextual information for programming on a second device.

Thought Leader: An individual or firm that is recognized as an authority in a specialized field and whose expertise is sought and rewarded.

Viewability: The concept of whether or not an advertisement that someone paid for was actually seen by a person in real life.

Viral: Describes how content quickly spreads throughout the Internet in much the same manner as a virus.

Terms

360 Campaign: Holistic promotion that covers all the bases, both online and offline, social media and more.

Analytics: The systematic computational analysis of data or statistics.

Campaign: A concerted marketing effort executed through a series of advertisements that share a message or theme.

Clickbait: Outlandish headlines designed for the sole purpose of driving clicks. These headlines are all bark and no bite, as the actual content rarely if ever lives up to the spectacular headline.

Click Fraud: A type of fraud that occurs in pay per click (PPC) advertising where a person, automated script or computer program imitates a legitimate user for the purpose of generating a charge per click with no actual interest in the ad's link.

Content Marketing: The marketing and business process for creating and distributing relevant and valuable content to attract, acquire, and engage a clearly defined and understood audience – with the objective of driving profitable customer action.

CPC: Cost-per-click is an online pricing model where an advertiser pays every time their ad is clicked.

CPM: Cost-per-thousand views is an online pricing model where an advertiser pays every for every one thousand times their ad is viewed. This pricing model works best branding or exposure is the objective rather than direct action.

CTR: Click-through-rate is a measure of how often an ad was clicked compared to how often it was shown (CTR= clicks/impressions).

Curator: A web user who ingests, analyzes and contextualizes content onto a platform or into a format the mainstream can understand.

Deep-linking: Using a hyperlink that links to a specific, generally searchable and indexed, piece of web content on a website rather than the home page.

Disruptors: Non-conformists who rock the boat; they change and/or challenge the way things are done (e.g. Netflix, Uber, Airbnb etc.)

Engagement: Strategies that brands use to foster relationships and the resulting online consumer actions, including likes and shares

Freemium: A pricing strategy where a basic version of a product or service is offered for free, with additional features and functionality requiring the user to upgrade to a paid version.

Geotargeting: Ad targeting based on a specific audience or demographics' physical location.

Ideation: The process of generating, developing and communicating new ideas.

Impressions: When your ad is viewable to be shown online.

Influencer Marketing: Focus is placed on a few key individuals (or types of individuals) as opposed to the target market as a whole with the hope that audience they garner will buy.

Inforgraphic: A graphical representation of information or data.

Keyword: A word or phrase used to match online content. Keywords are used to trigger search results or ads.

KPI: Key performance indicator, a success metric for your campaign.

Landing Page: The first page a person lands on after clicking an ad or link. Landing pages are designed to collect information and move visitors further into the site.

Match Type: Match types control which searches can trigger an ad. In Google Adwords the match types are exact, phrase, broad and broad modified.

Microsites: A web page or cluster or small cluster of pages meant to function within an existing website or to complement an offline activity.

Netiquette: The etiquette of the Internet.

PPC: Pay per click advertising where you pay every time your ad gets clicked on.

Real-time Engagement: Communicating with and building relationships with customers through active, real-time interactions (e.g. the SyFy Channel show *FaceOff* has you tweet your favorite makeup during the show using the #FaceOff hashtag to win prizes).

Remarketing (aka re-targeting): The slightly stalker-ish practice of showing users ads for a product or service they were viewing earlier.

ROI: Return on investment, shows how profitable an investment was.

SEM: Search engine marketing is the promotion of websites by increasing their visibility on search engine results pages (SERPs) through paid advertising.

SEO: Search engine optimization is the process of affecting the visibility of a website or a web page in a search engine's unpaid results – often referred to as "organic" or "natural" results.

SERPs: Search engine results pages are the pages that are returned after entering a search query into a search engine.

Trolls: Because they have miserable lives, these people deliberately posts provocative messages with the intent of causing maximum argument and disruption.

UGC: User generated content is defined as any form of content such as blogs, wikis, discussion forums, posts, chats, tweets, podcasting, pins, digital images, videos etc. that were created by the users of an online platform or service, oftentimes made available via social media.

Value Proposition: The intersection of the product/service and the customer's need.

Visual Storytelling: The practice of using visual assets (whether image or video) to tell a story.

Wearable Tech: Technology that is wearable on your person (e.g. Google Glass, FitBit, Apple Watch etc).

Adapted from the following sources:

Profoundry - Buzz or Bull? The Top 21 Buzzwords of 2014/2015
http://www.profoundry.co/top-21-digital-buzzwords-2014/

Mashable - 30 Overused Buzzwords in Digital Marketing
http://mashable.com/2013/05/23/buzzword-infographic/

WordStream - The Ultimate A-Z Marketing Buzzwords Bible
http://www.wordstream.com/blog/ws/2015/02/23/marketing-buzzwords

LinkedIn - Top 20 Digital Marketing Buzzwords You MUST Understand
https://www.linkedin.com/pulse/top-20-digital-marketing-buzzwords-you-must-marissa-ferraraccio

Content Marketing Institute - Six Useful Content Marketing Definitions
http://contentmarketinginstitute.com/2012/06/content-marketing-definition/

References:

1. Network Solutions, LLC. (1998, August 11). *Telecommuting Jobs & Professional Part-Time Jobs*. Retrieved from http://www.flexjobs.com/

2. CSC Corporate Domains, INC. (2006, April 06). *Workshifting – Anywhere is my office*. Retrieved from http://www.workshifting.com/

3. Citrix. (2006, April 06). *Workshifting: a global market research report*. Retrieved from https://www.citrix.com/content/dam/citrix/en_us/documents/news /workshifting-a-global-market-research-report.pdf

4. Osinubi, T. (2015, March 15). *5 reasons your 5 reasons may suck!* [Web log post]. Retrieved June 2, 2015 from http://consulttemi.com/5-reasons-your-5-reasons-may-suck/

5. Bass, S. (n.d.). *Top Web-Savvy Professors.* [Web log post]. Retrieved February 16, 2015 from http://bestonlineuniversities.com/web-savvy-professors/

6. NBC News. (2015, May 05). *Live-Streaming Apps Under Scrutiny After Mayweather-Pacquiao*. Retrieved from http://www.nbcnews.com/nightly-news/video/live-streaming-apps-under-scrutiny-after-mayweather-pacquiao-440298051681

7. Baer, J. (n.d.) *This chart explains the Reachpocalypse and why-*

Facebook is laughing all the way to the bank. [Web log post]. Retrieved May 13, 2015 from http://www.convinceandconvert.com/social-media-tools/this-chart-explains-the-reachpocalypse-and-why-facebook-is-laughing-all-the-way-to-the-bank/

8. Baer, J. (n.d.) *It's time to own your social community.* [Web log post]. Retrieved August 19, 2015 from http://www.convinceandconvert.com/social-media-strategy/its-time-to-own-your-social-community/

9. Burky, B. (2010, April 06). *About Brett | Radically Ambitious.* Retrieved May 13, 2015 from http://radicallyambitious.com/about-me-brett/

10. Mesh Digital Limited. (2009, May 03). *DistilledU – Online SEO University from Distilled.* Retrieved May 13, 2015 from https://www.distilled.net/u/

11. Google. (n.d.). *Learn with Google Webinars.* Retrieved May 13, 2015 from https://www.google.com/ads/experienced/webinars.html

12. Google. (2013, May). *Our Mobile Planet: United States of America.* Retrieved May 13, 2015 from https://think.withgoogle.com/databoard/media/pdfs/US_OurMobilePlanet_Research_English_2013_2.pdf

13. Peterson, T. (2014, November 04). *Digital to Overtake TV Ad Spending in Two Years, Says Forrester.* [Web log post]. Retrieved August 19, 2015 from http://adage.com/article/media/digital-overtake-tv-ad-spending-years-forrester/295694/

14. eMarketer. (2015, May 19). *U.S. Digital Ad Spending Will Approach $60 Billion This Year with Retailers Leading-Way.* [Web log post]. Retrieved August 19, 2015 from http://www.emarketer.com/Article/US-Digital-Ad-Spending-Will-Approach-60-Billion-This-Year-with-Retailers-Leading-Way/1012497

15. eMarketer. (2010, August 13). *Email Dominates Mobile Web Time.* [Web log post]. Retrieved August 19, 2015 from http://www.emarketer.com/Article/Email-Dominates-Mobile-Web-Time/1007868

16. Sebastian, M. (2015, March 24). *Marketers to Boost Global Ad Spending This Year to $540-billion.* [Web log post]. Retrieved August 19, 2015 from http://adage.com/article/media/marketers-boost-global-ad-spending-540-billion/297737/

17. Lunden, I. (2015, January 20). *2015 Ad Spend Rises To $187B, Digital Inches Closer To One Third Of It.* [Web log post]. Retrieved August 19, 2015 from http://techcrunch.com/2015/01/20/2015-ad-spend-rises-to-187b-digital-inches-closer-to-one-third-of-it/

18. Hickman, G. (n.d.) *Mobile Stats & Usage Data*. Retrieved May 13, 2015 from http://mobilemarketingengine.com/stats/

19. Hickman, G. (n.d.) *16 Mobile Stats You Can't Ignore*. Retrieved May 13, 2015 from http://mobilemarketingengine.com/16-mobile-marketing-stats-you-cant-ignore/

20. O'Malley, G. (2012, March 26). *Localized Creative Improves Click-Through Rates, Engagement.* [Web log post]. Retrieved August 19, 2015 from http://www.mediapost.com/publications/article/171106/localized-creative-improves-click-through-rates-e.html

21. Statista. (n.d.) *Mobile retail commerce sales in the United States from 2013 to 2019 (in billion U.S. dollars)*. Retrieved May 13, 2015 from http://www.statista.com/statistics/249855/mobile-retail-commerce-revenue-in-the-united-states/

22. CMO Council. (n.d.) *Mobile Marketing*. Retrieved May 13, 2015 from https://www.cmocouncil.org/facts-stats-categories.php?view=all&category=mobile-marketing

About the Authors

Michelle A Bassett

Michelle A. Bassett is a born entrepreneur and a highly skilled Internet Marketer. She uses her unmatched analytical and deductive reasoning skills to creatively craft campaigns around her clients needs. Ms. Bassett has an extensive background in SEO, PPC, Funnel Creation and Social Media Marketing. This experience has afforded her a track record of highly successful marketing campaigns. Starting from humble beginnings, Ms. Bassett stays community conscious. Despite her early environment, she made the commitment to take her education to never before seen heights. With a bachelors degree in Behavior Analysis and a Master Degree in Internet Marketing, not only did she become the first person in her family to graduate from college, but she has become an unstoppable force in the Internet Marketing community.

Stay Connected:

http://StartMarketingWithMichelle.com

Twitter: @CEOMichelleB

LinkedIn: www.linkedin.com/in/michelleb6

Temitayo A. Osinubi

Mr. Osinubi holds the distinction of graduating Salutatorian from Full Sail University's Internet Marketing Bachelor of Science (IMBS) program. Through coursework he's developed a strong understanding of all things Digital Marketing with an emphasis on mobile marketing. He also has experience in managing interactive, digital and mobile programs of various complexities.

A dynamic speaker, Mr. Osinubi's presentation style captivates an audience while delivering actionable insights. He strikes a delicate balance between candor and humor that is engaging and hard to beat. Mr. Osinubi brings the trained eye and mindset of an investor to Internet Marketing, making his uniquely suited to both spot and leverage Digital Marketing opportunities. Mr. Osinubi is a consummate professional with a track record of success.

Stay connected:

http://ConsultTemi.com

Twitter: @tembo8482

LinkedIn: www.linkedin.com/in/temitayoaosinubi

www.ingramcontent.com/pod-product-compliance
Lightning Source LLC
Chambersburg PA
CBHW021227090426
42740CB00006B/416